ROBERT

and the 35th STAR
the

by Tim McKinney

PICTORIAL HISTORIES PUBLISHING COMPANY, INC.
4103 Virginia Avenue, SE, Charleston, W.Va. 25304

LIBRARY OF CONGRESS
CATALOG CARD NUMBER 93-084769

ISBN 0-929521-75-7

First Printing July 1993

Typography: Leslie R. Maricelli
Layout: Stan Cohen
Cover Graphics: Mike Egeler

PICTORIAL HISTORIES PUBLISHING CO., INC.
4103 Virginia Avenue, S.E., Charleston, W.Va. 25304

INTRODUCTION

Often misunderstood and frequently overlooked, the campaigns of the Civil War in West Virginia deserve fresh study. In this work I have attempted to present a balanced view of the military, and to a lesser extent, the political events of 1861, which ultimately led to the addition of West Virginia as the 35th state in the Union. For purposes of clarity I have referred to "West" Virginia in 1861, although statehood was not achieved until June 20, 1863.

Supplementing the text are 21 maps which I believe will assist the reader in understanding the many troop movements and battles as they developed. For general reference it is recommended the reader refer to the large two-page map at the front of the book.

The military campaigns of eastern Virginia and other theaters of the war, eventually cast the West Virginia campaigns into obscurity. That has truly been an historical injustice. The eyes of the country, and even of the world, were focused on West Virginia in 1861 as the first theater of the war. News from West Virginia was as sought after in those early days of conflict, as it would later be from anywhere else in the country. The military activity here was neither glorious nor bloodthirsty. It was however, arduous almost beyond description, and it left upon the minds of the participants a lasting impression of the privations and hardships of mountain warfare. Many of those who first felt the pain of war in West Virginia, and later participated in bloody and difficult campaigns elsewhere, would write that at no time during the war did their hardships exceed those of the West Virginia campaign.

I hope I have done their memory, and their sacrifices, justice. We owe them all, Blue & Gray, an honored place in our nation's history.

Dedicated to the people of West Virginia
—verily the land of Canaan—

Tim McKinney
March 24, 1993

ACKNOWLEDGMENTS

This is my fifth history publication in as many years, and if the experience has left me with one overriding impression, it is the great sense of debt which I feel to so many people, near and far, whose kind assistance has helped make these works possible. I have attempted here to acknowledge everyone who contributed directly or indirectly, to this project. Of these, several people or institutions merit special mention:

William R. Erwin, Jr. of the William R. Perkins Library, Duke University, Durham, NC. Mr. Erwin and the entire Special Collections Staff at Duke University assisted me much more via the mail than any researcher has a right to expect.

Joe Geiger, Jr. of Huntington, W.Va. who unselfishly shared with me his considerable research into the battles of Bartow and Allegheny Mountain, West Virginia.

Bill McNeel of Marlinton, W.Va. who, in response to a single inquiry, sent me a large and helpful packet of old newspaper articles, photographs, and other materials relating to the war in Randolph and Pocahontas Counties. Bill also made time in his busy schedule to give me an off-season tour of the excellent Pocahontas County Historical Society Museum at Marlinton, W.Va. in 1991.

Otis K. Rice of Hugheston, W.Va. a valued friend and mentor, who has given his life to the study and preservation of West Virginia history. Dr. Rice is truly a jewel of the 35th Star.

Tony Wappel of the Special Collections Division, University Libraries, University of Arkansas, Fayetteville. Mr. Wappel patiently tolerated my numerous letters and telephone requests for information. His generosity in locating materials relevant to the Third Arkansas Infantry, is gratefully acknowledged.

A belated thank you to all of the educators who managed, even from my youth, to ignite in me the flames of curiosity which have carried me across the years. Education and opportunity to learn can be a virtual anchor in an age of decadence.

And a heartfelt thank you to the following: Mrs. Juanita E. Allen, President, Mary Custis Lee 17th Va. Regiment, Chapter No. 7, United Daughters of the Confederacy, Alexandria, Va; Angela Allison, Lee Headquarters Trust, Inc. Ronceverte, W.Va.; Fred Armstrong, W.Va. Dept. of Culture and History, Charleston; Pete and Phyllis Baxter, Rich Mountain Battlefield Foundation, Inc., P.O. Box 227, Beverly, W.Va., 26253. Bob and Cristine Beckelheimer, Oak Hill, W.Va.; Carolyn Campbell, Vining Library, West Virginia Tech, Montgomery; Stan Cohen, Pictorial

Histories Publishing Co., Missoula, Mt. and Charleston, W.Va.; Dennis Deitz, Mountain Memories Press, S.Charleston, W.Va.; Harold Forbes, W.Va. Regional History Collection, Colson Hall, WVU, Morgantown; Phyllis Gray, Midland Trail Scenic Highway Association, Jodie, W.Va.; Sen. Bob Holliday, Fayetteville, W.Va.; Terry Lowry, S.Charleston, W.Va.; Karen Peters, Mount Vernon Ladies Association, Mt. Vernon, Va; Mike and Margaret Smith, Droop Mt. State Park, Hillsboro, W.Va.; Frances Swope, Greenbrier Co. Historical Society, Lewisburg, W.Va.; Steve Thomas, Thomas-In-Prints, Gauley Bridge, W.Va.; Karen Vuranch, National Trust For Historic Preservation, Mt. Hope, W.Va.; Noble Wyatt, Kanawha Valley Civil War Round Table, Poca, W.Va..

Institutions providing assistance and not already mentioned include: The Indiana Historical Society, Indianapolis; the Oberlin College Archives, Oberlin, Ohio; the Cincinnati Historical Society, Cincinnati; the Ohio Historical Society, (Glen Longacre and Jeff Thomas) Columbus; the Virginia Historical Society and the Virginia State Library, Richmond; Virginia Military Institute Archives, Lexington; Washington & Lee University, Lexington, Va.; the Georgia State Archives, Atlanta; the Kentucky Historical Society, Frankfort; the Mississippi State Archives, Jackson; the Tennessee State Archives & Library, Nashville; the entire staff of the West Virginia Department of Culture & History, Charleston, and all of my family and friends, with special notice of the late Mike Pauley, formerly with the West Virginia Historic Preservation Office. Mike died suddenly in 1992, but his legacy survives in the form of his excellent work to preserve and promote state history. He was a good friend and fellow historian whose cordial ways and many talents are sadly missed.

Fairmont

Grafton

Oakland

Upper Potomac

Phillippi

Laurel Mountain

hannon

Beverly

Huttonsville

Mountains

State Boundary

Harri

Staunton

Virginia

Covington

West Virginia

he Kanawha Campaigns in 1861-1862

Scale — 30 Miles

5   10   15   20   25

Wagonroads-----------
Railroads....................

TABLE OF CONTENTS

Francis H. Pierpont
Loyal Governor of Virginia, 1861-1868

BALLOTS AND BULLETS

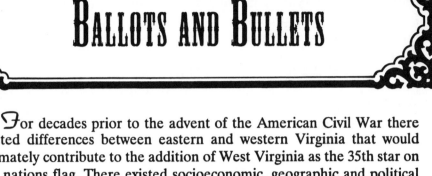

𝒵or decades prior to the advent of the American Civil War there existed differences between eastern and western Virginia that would ultimately contribute to the addition of West Virginia as the 35th star on our nations flag. There existed socioeconomic, geographic and political differences which included the disbursement of funds garnered from taxes. Many residents of western Virginia felt that the balance of tax expenditures favored the east, thus depriving them of adequate funds for internal improvements such as road construction. Some contemporary accounts of the east/west situation offer additional insight. One writer observed that "From the nature of its earlier settlement, and by reason of climate, soil and situation, Eastern Virginia remained the region of large plantations, with a heavy slave population, and of profitable agriculture, especially in the production of tobacco. West Virginia, on the contrary, having been first settled by hunters, pioneers, lumbermen and miners, possessed little in common with her more wealthy and aristocratic neighbors beyond the mountains."[1]

Thus there would seem to have existed two Virginia's even before our great Civil War and the calamitous events which came in its wake. Eastern Virginia's economy in 1860 was largely slave-based, while the "peculiar institution" was less in evidence in the transmontane counties. With news of Abraham Lincoln's election as president reverberating across the South, 94 members of the Virginia General Assembly met with Gov. John Letcher to devise a plan of action. Lincoln was against the expansion of slavery beyond the areas where it already existed, and it was thus feared in the South that only non-slaveholding states would be admitted to the Union under Lincoln, effectively altering the balance of power toward the North.

On Nov. 15, 1860, Governor Letcher issued a proclamation calling the General Assembly into extra session on Jan. 7, 1861. "Great excitement prevails in the public mind," he said, "and prudence requires that the representatives of the people of this Commonwealth should ... determine calmly and wisely what action is necessary in this emergency."[2]

Eastern Virginia began promoting States' Rights and debating whether or not to secede from the Union, while at the same time Virginia's Northwestern counties endeavored to avoid secession. Unionists meetings sprang up in numerous Northwestern counties. Resolutions condemning secession and calling for division of the state resulted from these meetings, with Unionists in Tyler County declaring that if Virginia voted to secede from the Union, they would be "in favor of striking West Virginia from Eastern Virginia and forming a state independent of the South, and firm to the Union." [3]

In assessing the Union sentiment that existed in West Virginia during this period, one should not construe the ultimate division of western from eastern Virginia to mean that the west possessed an overwhelming Northern bias; it did not. In his excellent monograph *A House Divided*, published in 1964, Dr. Richard Orr Curry argues effectively that 25 of 50 counties encompassed by West Virginia supported the Confederacy and opposed division of the Commonwealth. Dr. Curry explains that those counties "Comprised nearly two-thirds of the total area of this state and they contained 142,000 white inhabitants or 40 percent of the total population. Northwestern Union counties, though smaller in size, had approximately 210,000 people. The Rebel minority ran as high as 40 percent in some Union counties; but the reverse was also true. Therefore, a 60-40 split favorable to Unionists appears to be accurate in gauging the loyalties of inhabitants included in this state." [4]

Based on this and other more recent research, it would seem evident that West Virginia as a bastion of Nationalism or Union solidarity is a myth.[5] Thus we begin to see that the political situation which General Lee and his Confederates found in West Virginia, though not ideal, was none the less more amicable to the Southern Confederacy than most historians would have us believe.

Between the date of Lincoln's election to the presidency and his inauguration on March 4, 1861, political turmoil and debate was rampant not only in Virginia, but nationwide. In the ensuing months it quickly became obvious that Virginia would join her sister states in the South and secede from the Union. Equally obvious was the fact that in response to that act West Virginia would secede from Virginia. The question was not so much if, but how and when.

On April 17, 1861, Virginia adopted the Ordinance of Secession, which in turn expedited efforts already underway to form the "Loyal Government" of Virginia, in the west. From Clarksburg resolutions calling for a general convention at Wheeling on May 13, 1861, were quickly circulated. The convention was to determine the course of action "the people of Northwestern Virginia should take in the present fearful emergency." [6]

Less than one week after the Secession Convention General Lee was ordered to take command of "all the military and naval forces of the

State and take in charge the military defenses of the state." Subsequently, on April 29, 1861, Lee ordered Col. John McCausland to "proceed to the valley of the Kanawha, and muster into the service of the State such volunteer companies ... as may offer their services .... take command of them, and direct the military operations for the protection of that section of country .... and you are desired to report what points below Charleston will most effectually accomplish the objects in view." [7]

Also on April 29, Lee ordered Maj. A. Loring to gather what volunteer forces he could and "direct the military operations for the protection of the terminus of the Baltimore and Ohio Railroad on the Ohio River .... Maj. F.M. Boykin, Jr., has been directed to give protection to the road in the vicinity of Grafton .... " [8]

It was readily apparent to both governments, North and South, that

having military control over Northwestern Virginia would prove critical to offense or defense. Confederate authorities at Richmond knew that with secession the area of Virginia west of the Allegheny's stood isolated and open to invasion. From the outset both governments hoped to control West Virginia's Baltimore and Ohio Railroad, an important east-west link. In addition, there were four important turnpikes which would be useful in moving armies and equipment. The areas' many farms which produced beef, wheat, and corn, were also valuable, as were the highly productive salt works of the Kanawha Valley. Furthermore, if the Union could hold West Virginia one of the Confederacy's most prized states would be split. On the other hand, the South hoped to show strength and solidarity by keeping Virginia intact.

Gen. Robert E. Lee in early 1861.

Attempting to recruit Confederate troops in the area of Weston and preparing to defend Grafton, Maj. Francis Boykin received orders from General Lee dated April 30, 1861, instructing him to "Assume the command, take post at or near Grafton ... for the command of the Baltimore and Ohio Railroad and the branch to Parkersburg .... to hold the road for the benefit of Maryland and Virginia, and to prevent its being used against them .... Maj. A. Loring, at Wheeling, has been directed...to give protection to the road near its terminus at the Ohio River .... Please state whether a force at Parkersburg will be necessary, and what number of companies can be furnished in that vicinity .... two hundred muskets of the old pattern, flint-locks, will be forwarded by Colonel Jackson, the commanding officer at Harpers Ferry."[9]

Although West Virginia would send an estimated 20,000 troops to the Confederacy over the duration of the war, Lee, Jefferson Davis, former Virginia Gov. Henry Wise, and other Southern leaders, would initially underestimate the difficulties they faced in recruiting and supplying troops in the west. They also overestimated the speed with which men could be enlisted, and the numbers that would enlist. Recruitment efforts so distant from Richmond were meager at best. It is interesting to note that in Lee's order to Major Boykin on April 30, he asked "whether a force at Parkersburg will be necessary." Had Lee fully grasped the pro-Union sentiment in extreme Northwestern Virginia, he certainly would not have asked a question that with the benefit of hindsight appears, for General Lee, uncharacteristically ignorant. Not only would a "force at Parkersburg" be necessary, but that entire section of Northwestern Virginia would be in firm Union control within a few weeks of Lee's inquiry.

On May 4, Lee sent orders to Col. George A. Porterfield, who was then at Harpers Ferry, instructing him to proceed to Grafton and prepare for defense of the Baltimore and Ohio Railroad and that section of Virginia. Lee explained that Major Loring was in command at Wheeling, with a volunteer force, and that Major Boykin was already at work mustering volunteers in the area and would follow Colonel Porterfield's orders. Lee also told Porterfield that he was authorized to extend the call for volunteers "to the Counties of Wood, Wirt, Roane, Calhoun, Gilmer, Ritchie, Pleasant, and Doddridge to rendezvous at Parkersburg, and to the Counties of Braxton, Lewis, Harrison, Monongalia, Taylor, Barbour, Upshur, Tucker, Marion, Randolph, and Preston to rendezvous at Grafton." Lee further explained that he did not know what number of companies might offer their services, but that he "supposed that a regiment composed of infantry, riflemen, and artillery, may be obtained for the Parkersburg Branch." [10]

A few days later, and before Colonel Porterfield had time to arrive, General Lee received from Major Boykin a long and disconcerting letter stating that results of Confederate recruitment efforts in the vicinity of

Grafton were very unfavorable. On May 11, Lee responded, telling Boykin that he "must persevere, however, and call out companies from the well affected counties, and march them to Grafton or such other point in that vicinity as you may select. Four hundred rifles and some ammunition have been ordered from Staunton to Major Goff...at Beverly, Randolph County, who has been directed to communicate their arrival to Colonel Porterfield ... You can by this means arm certain companies ... preparatory to receiving those from Harper's Ferry." [11]

Writing from Grafton on May 16, Colonel Porterfield informed the Confederate Adjutant General at Richmond that for reasons unknown to him the arms and ammunition said to be in route to him had never arrived. He stated that several companies had been assembled in the area and that he had "sent orders to the captains of the companies, supposed to be armed, in the surrounding counties to bring their companies immediately to a point near Grafton." To Porterfield's dismay, he soon found that almost all of the companies which had been recruited were entirely without weapons. "This is a serious disappointment" he said, stating that he had been told companies were organizing at Pruntytown, Philippi, and Clarksburg, but that they were all without arms and uniforms. He said that even after this force was assembled it would not "for some months be more effective than undisciplined militia." Also that there was one company at Weston and another at Fairmont armed with "old flint-lock muskets, in bad order, and no ammunition .... now marching toward this point" Commenting on the reception he received at Grafton he said he "found great diversity of opinion and much bitterness of feeling among the people of this region." [12]

Confederate efforts in the Kanawha Valley were progressing somewhat better than in the northern counties with Col. John McCausland and Col. Christopher Q. Tompkins in command of the "Army of the Kanawha" while Porterfield's command was designated as the "Army of the Northwest." As the war progressed names and boundaries changed and the area fell successively within the Department of Southwestern Virginia, the trans-Allegheny or Western Department of Virginia, and the Department of Western Virginia and East Tennessee.

West Virginia would not long be held for the Confederacy. Federal troops under overall command of Gen. George B. McClellan began in early May concentrating at points along the Ohio River opposite Wheeling and Parkersburg, and at the mouth of the Kanawha River (Point Pleasant). In addition, a number of West Virginia Union Army companies had already been assembled in the vicinity of Wheeling and the northern panhandle, and Unionists held a convention at Wheeling from May 13 to 15, which was another ominous note to the Southern Confederacy. [13]

On May 26, General McClellan issued a "Proclamation to the People

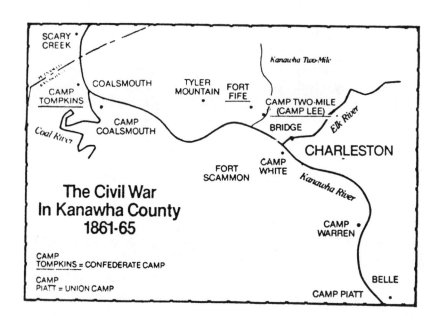

The Civil War
In Kanawha County
1861-65

CAMP TOMPKINS = CONFEDERATE CAMP

CAMP PIATT = UNION CAMP

of Western Virginia," saying that armed traitors were destroying the property of citizens of Virginia and ruining their railways, while also attempting to manipulate their political freedom. McClellan declared that the "great mass" of West Virginian's were loyal to the Union and that in response to their pleas for help he had ordered troops to cross the Ohio River. "They come as your friends and brothers" he said, "enemies only to the armed rebels who are preying upon you." To alleviate fears some had that the true aim of the Federal troops was to free their slaves, he told the people to "understand one thing clearly—not only will we abstain from all such interference, but we will, on the contrary, with an iron hand, crush any attempt at insurrection on their part." [14]

In an address to his troops also on May 26, McClellan told them they were "ordered to cross the frontier and enter upon the soil of Virginia. Your mission is to restore peace and confidence, to protect the majesty of the law, and to rescue our brethren from the grasp of armed traitors .... remember that your only foes are the armed traitors...when the loyal men of Western Virginia have been enabled to organize and arm, they can protect themselves, and you can then return to your homes with the proud satisfaction of having preserved a gallant people from destruction." [15]

Thus the die was cast, the invasion launched, and Virginia forever changed. Assisted by the 1st and 2nd West Virginia Infantry Regiments from Wheeling, McClellan's army proceeded south along the Baltimore and Ohio Railroad. Simultaneously the 14th and 18th Ohio Regiments

Gen. and Mrs. George B. McClellan about 1861.

occupied Parkersburg. Col. B.F. Kelley, commander of the 1st West Virginia Infantry, led the troops marching south from Wheeling. As he approached Fairmont, Colonel Porterfield, commanding the Confederate troops, withdrew his men to Philippi, temporarily placing a distance of 35 miles between his force and the Yankees. [16]

By the evening of June 2, the Federal Army had consolidated their forces within easy striking distance of the Confederates at Philippi, and in the early morning hours of June 3, they attacked Colonel Porterfield's command. Surprised and outnumbered, the Confederates fled in chaos. The entire affair lasted but a few minutes, and the first land battle of the Civil War proved to be an inglorious Southern defeat dubbed the "Philippi Races." [17]

The Confederates retreated all the way to Beverly, Randolph County, and from there notified the authorities at Richmond of their predicament: "Our troops at Philippi have been attacked by a large force with artillery under McClelland and drew back to Beverly. We must have as large a number of troops as possible from Richmond without a moments delay or else abandon the Northwest." [18]

Gen. Robert S. Garnett was sent to take command of the Army of the Northwest, arriving in Randolph County on June 14. The situation that General Garnett found there was not a pleasant one. The Southern sol-

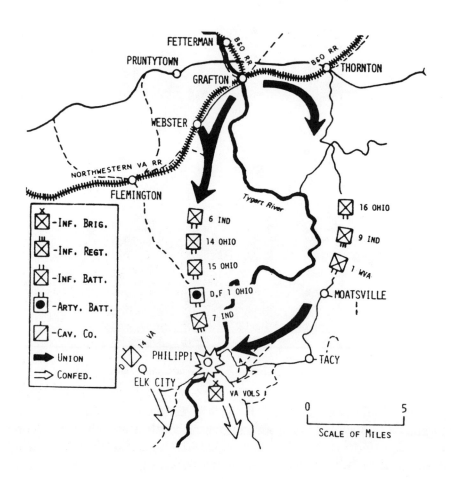

The Battle at Philippi, Va., June 3, 1861.

diers and many civilians were demoralized by the Philippi defeat. Compounding their problems was a chronic shortage of supplies and insufficient training for the troops. There also seemed to be no cohesive plan of defense for the region. After inspecting the camps at Beverly and Huttonsville, Garnett established his headquarters at nearby Laurel Hill (Bealington). A few days later he wrote to General Lee who was still in Richmond, informing him of the state of affairs in the west: "I found there (Huttonsville) 23 companies of infantry ... in a most miserable condition as to arms, clothing, equipment, instruction, and discipline .... I deemed it of such importance to possess the two turnpike passes over the Rich and Laurel Mountains, before they should be seized by the enemy ... that with two regiments and Captain Rice's battery ... marching them a greater portion of the night, reached the two passes early in the afternoon of the following day .... I regard these two passes as the gates to the northwestern country ..." [19]

General Lee urged Garnett to destroy the Cheat River Bridge over the Baltimore and Ohio Railroad but Garnett feared that his meager force of approximately 3,000 troops would not be equal to the task. His fears were not unfounded as General McClellan had upwards of 20,000 men at his disposal with which to oppose the Confederates. Though Garnett's Army of the Northwest would eventually exceed 4,000 troops, it would prove to be too little too late.

General McClellan arrived in Grafton on June 21, to take personal

Gen. Robert Garnett, C.S.A.

command of operations against Garnett. Writing to his wife on the day of his arrival about the reception he had received along his route, McClellan told her that crowds had assembled to see him and cheer him in his mission, saying "I never went through such a scene in my life." [20]

Announcing to the troops that he had arrived on the scene, McClellan said he had "heard that there was danger here. I have come to place myself at your head and share it with you. I fear now but one thing—that you will not find foemen worthy of your steel." [21] McClellan's letter was written at Buckhannon, a community distant some 25 miles from Rich Mountain, a position from which he would later launch an offensive against Garnett's command.

Concerned about developments in the west, Confederate authorities at Richmond ordered former Virginia Gov. Henry A. Wise into the Kanawha Valley, with orders to assume command. Wise was strictly a "political general" with no military experience, and this fact would prove to be yet another nail in the Confederate coffin. Traveling the James River and Kanawha Turnpike he reached Gauley Bridge, about 40 miles east of Charleston, on June 22. Wise found the Army of the Kanawha in no better shape than General Garnett had found his Army of the Northwest, eight days earlier.

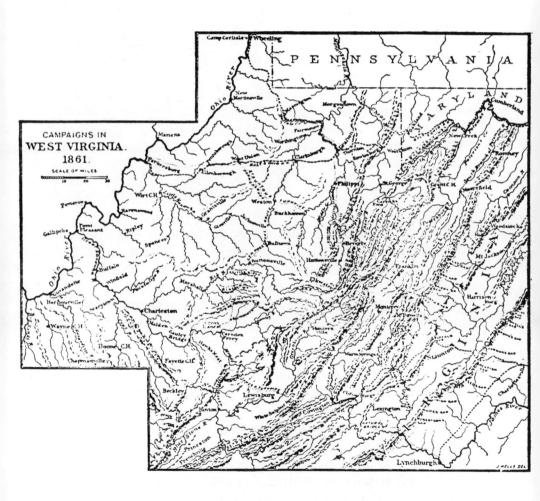

CAMPAIGNS IN
WEST VIRGINIA.
1861.

SCALE OF MILES

On June 23, Wise wrote to Col. C.Q. Tompkins, who was still attempting to recruit and train troops in the western Kanawha Valley with headquarters at Coalsmouth, (present-day St. Albans) near Charleston. Wise told Tompkins that he had found only about 430 men at Gauley Bridge and vicinity, and that he would be advancing to Charleston the next day with about "300 efficient men, well armed." [22] General Wise arrived at Charleston, Kanawha County, on Wednesday, June 26, establishing his headquarters at a local hotel known as the "Kanawha House."

As Wise occupied Charleston, McClellan was consolidating his forces at several strategic points in the Northwest. He concentrated about 8,000 men at Buckhannon, with 4,000 men at Philippi under command of Brig. Gen. T.A. Morris, whose men had been for a number of days engaged in minor skirmishes with Confederate troops at Laurel Hill. General McClellan had additional men at other points including Weston, Clarksburg, Bulltown, and Grafton.

As the Federal troops were positioning themselves for a strong surge southward, General Wise accurately determined that any invasion of the western Kanawha Valley would necessarily come, at least in part, south from Marietta, Ohio, via Parkersburg, Ravenswood, and Ripley, on to Charleston. Accordingly, on June 29, Wise dispatched a force of 800 men to Ripley, 38 miles northwest of Charleston, with orders to occupy Ripley and any other points which circumstances might allow. Wise's men arrived at Ripley tired and hungry on June 30, and as word of their advance had preceded them any Union troops that may have been in the vicinity were entirely absent. After scouting the

Gen. Henry A. Wise, C.S.A.
1806-1876

area and posting sufficient pickets the Virginian's encamped in and about the court house. The following day Confederates pushed westward another three miles toward the Ohio River. They had received information that Federal troops were entrenched at Cottage Mills, (present day Cottageville) and they determined to make the attack. Advancing cautiously Southern troops reached their destination but, to their dismay, found nary a Yankee in sight. After scouting the area briefly they began the return to Ripley and were attacked rather half-heartedly by a small band of Unionist militia. This minor engagement apparently resulted in no casualties to either side though the feisty Confederates enjoyed the sound of gunfire and smell of smoke, brief though it was. [23]

General McClellan was well aware of the enemy movements about Ripley, and on July 1, he ordered an advance on that community by the 17th and 21st Ohio Infantry Regiment's. The two regiments united at Ravenswood, 14 miles north of Ripley, at 11 p.m. July 3, and resumed their march southward. The anxious Yankee's would find no enemy however, as the Southerners were then marching back toward the Kanawha Valley. General Wise apparently did not approve of their return at this time, and on July 4, he personally joined his "Ripley task force," finding them at Sissonville, some 10 miles north of Charleston.[24] Wise hoped to quickly reoccupy Ripley and so he ordered his weary soldiers back on the road before midnight of July 5. The night was cool and rainy, certainly not well suited to a forced march, and though the Confederates did stop to rest it was altogether a difficult trek, as one participant later recalled: "a tedious journey through the rain ... spent another night at Scofford, or rather from two in the morning until daylight ... lay down on the wet ground, where I was nearly devoured by fleas ... rose at daylight ... without breakfast reached Ripley at 11 a.m."[25] As luck would have it the two adversaries would again fail to clash. Finding no Confederates at Ripley, the Federal forces had returned to Ravenswood.

Fearing that the Federal forces at and near Gallipolis, Ohio, would soon attack into the Kanawha Valley and find the Confederate army divided, Colonel Tompkins began to ask Wise to return. General Wise however had determined to stand his ground and he told Tompkins that he believed Ripley to be a "far more important position than I deemed it before coming here." Wise added that he intended to erect earthworks in the vicinity to "prevent entire occupation of this road and the roads eastward, by the enemy, both from Ravenswood and Parkersburg." Wise also explained that he hoped to render impassable the road "leading to this place from Parkersburg, Ravenswood, and that from the Ohio, via Mill Creek." There was however a "fly in Wise's ointment," in that he had no tools with which to construct the works he wanted. Explaining this oversight to Tompkins, Wise said "There is not a mattock, spade, or pick axe to be got here. If, to be got at Charleston send a few to Ripley immediately."[26]

Seeing the foolishness in having an already numerically inferior army divided, Colonel Tompkins continued to plead with his commander to return. Finally, on July 8, General Wise commenced his return to Charleston, reaching camp there on Wednesday, July 10. His adventure northward had been largely uneventful, although a 160 man detachment of his cavalry had clashed with members of the 17th Indiana Infantry at Glenville, Gilmer County, on July 7. Upon his return Wise was greeted with a report from E.J. Harvie, Assistant Adjutant General of the Wise Legion, which left no doubt as to the poor state of the Legion. Wise's total command was listed as just 2,863 men. The report also concluded that the troops were entirely without the supplies and equipment necessary to wage war, and that they were led by incompetent officers. Adjutant Harvie also said that in their present condition "but little is to be expected from them and whenever brought into collision with a disciplined force it were unwise to rely upon them for attack or defense ...." You can imagine how such a report as that must have deflated the old governor's ego, at least temporarily! [27]

In the Northwest General Garnett received reports from citizens and his own scouts that an overwhelming Union force was massing to attack his positions. On July 1, and again on July 6, Garnett wrote to Lt. Col. George Deas, Assistant Adjutant and Inspector General, saying that he believed the Kanawha Valley was mostly loyal to the South and that General Wise's Army of the Kanawha should attack Weston and Buckhannon to relieve pressure from the Army of the Northwest. Not satisfied with the response he got from Lieutenant Colonel Deas, Garnett wrote directly to Robert E. Lee with the same request, saying that Wise could march east and then northward via Summersville and Bulltown to attack Weston. In this manner Garnett felt that the Federal Army would fear losing possession of the Northwestern Railroad and adjacent country, and would thus be too occupied to attack his army or to invade the Kanawha Valley.

Not having full knowledge of the situation then facing General Wise, Lee wrote to him on July 11, advising him of Garnett's plan. Apparently Lee had concluded, again in absence of complete information, that General Garnett's idea did have some merit. Lee explained the plan to Wise in detail, adding: "... should you not find employment for your command in the Kanawha Valley, and think it advisable, you might concert measures with General Garnett for a united attack on the forces of General McClellan." [27]

Not only would Wise "find employment" for his army in the Kanawha Valley, but on the same date that Lee wrote to him, General McClellan would initiate a precise multi-level attack against both the Army of the Kanawha and the Army of the Northwest.

On July 2, McClellan ordered Gen. Jacob D. Cox to proceed to Gallipolis, Ohio, with 3,000 men, and prepare an invasion of the Kanawha Valley. At the same time, in the Northwest, McClellan held in readiness 12,000 men positioned at Buckhannon and Philippi, with additional forces in the surrounding communities. Opposing McClellan in the Northwest were about 1,300 Confederates at Rich Mountain, commanded by Lt. Col. John Pegram, and approximately 3,000 men entrenched at Laurel Hill some 12 miles from Rich Mountain, and commanded by General Garnett. Opposing General Cox in the Kanawha Valley was Wise and his Legion or Army of the Kanawha, now boasting 3,500 men of all arms, infantry, cavalry and artillery. Included among the officers assisting General Wise were two graduates of V.M.I., Col. John McCausland, and Capt. George S. Patton (grandfather of General Patton of WWII fame). Col. C.Q. Tompkins was also a capable military man, being an 1836 graduate of West Point Military Academy.

For Wise, however, the prior military experience of a handful of his officers would not offset the fact that he commanded a poorly trained and woefully equipped army. On July 11, a Union invasion force under General Cox began making its way up the Kanawha Valley from Point Pleasant. Federal troops were moving up the valley in a three-pronged enveloping movement. The 2nd Kentucky Infantry entered by way of the mouth of Guyandotte River; the 1st Kentucky Infantry moved from Ravenswood to strike Wise's base; while the main army moved up the Kanawha River on four light steamboats. Union cavalry took the advance, riding along the river banks, scouting and serving as a guard for the Federal wagon train.[28] The advancing columns met only light Confederate resistance and proceeded up the valley. A number of small skirmishes developed along the way, culminating in a battle at Scary Creek, Putnam County, on July 17. In that fight both sides withdrew from the battlefield, and after the smoke cleared Confederate commanders realized the situation and returned to claim a victory. Union casualties were 15 killed and nine wounded. The Confederates had four killed and six wounded. [29]

Though Southern forces were victorious at Scary Creek, it became obvious to General Wise that his position in the middle Kanawha Valley was untenable in the absence of reinforcements and supplies. With Cox's troops moving up the valley and additional Union forces under orders to march from the upper Tygart Valley region, via Weston, Sutton, and Bulltown, to cut the Southern lines at Gauley Bridge, Wise knew he would be caught between two jaws of a pincer movement. He sent a hurried dispatch to General Lee informing him of the situation and saying that his Legion was almost without ammunition. Seeing no viable option Wise ordered a retreat from the valley which began on July 24, among much confusion and calamity. Wise reached Gauley Bridge on the 26th and the

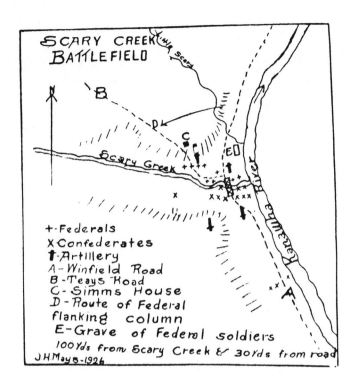

SCARY CREEK
BATTLEFIELD

+ -Federals
X -Confederates
↑ -Artillery
A - Winfield Road
B - Teays Road
C - Simms House
D - Route of Federal
flanking column
E - Grave of Federal soldiers
100 Yds from Scary Creek & 30 Yds from road
J.H.Mays-1926

next day he ordered the bridge there destroyed. Continuing his retreat southward, Wise arrived at Bungers Mill, a few miles west of Lewisburg, Greenbrier County, on July 31. The next day he sent a detailed explanation of his withdrawal and subsequent events to General Lee. He told Lee that the "Kanawha Valley is wholly disaffected and traitorous. It was gone from Charleston to Point Pleasant before I got there .... You cannot persuade these people that Virginia can or ever will reconquer the northwest, and they are submitting, subdued, and debased." [30]

The situation for Garnett's army was even more catastrophic over this same period, as General McClellan had ordered an attack at Rich Mountain at the same time Cox was moving up the Kanawha Valley. During the night of July 10, and early hours of the 11th, a heavy rain fell in the northwest and under those unfavorable conditions a Federal force of 1,917 men led by Gen. William S. Rosecrans, began a difficult and dangerous 10 mile march to flank the Confederate position at Rich Mountain. Suspecting that an attack was imminent Colonel Pegram had detached 350 men from his main camp on the western base of Rich Mountain, to positions near the road at the summit. This detachment

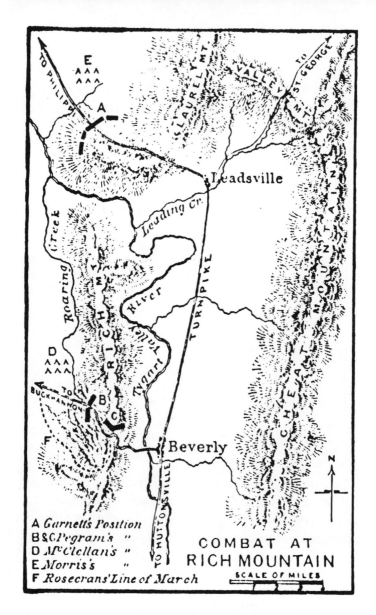

A *Garnett's Position*
B & C *Pegram's "*
D *McClellan's "*
E *Morris's "*
F *Rosecrans' Line of March*

COMBAT AT
RICH MOUNTAIN

SCALE OF MILES

encountered General Rosecrans' troops at 2:30 p.m. July 11, and a brisk fight ensued. The Federal's had been guided on their flank march by a young man named Hart, who lived on Rich Mountain, and whose farm bore the brunt of the battle. The turnpike at the Hart farm ran in a depression of the summit making the farm itself a more defensible position than was some of the surrounding area. It was here that Pegram's brave Confederates made their best stand, fending off their anxious adversaries for three bloody hours. Finally, a charge by part of the Union line, aided by some of their riflemen who had gained a good position, broke the Southerners from their ground just before nightfall.

Scattered and confused in the mountain darkness, Pegram and the remnants of his command decided to attempt to join Garnett at Laurel Hill. Daybreak of July 12, found the Confederates gone from the summit and from their main camp at the western foot of the mountain. A jubilant General Rosecrans sent a messenger to McClellan giving him the news that

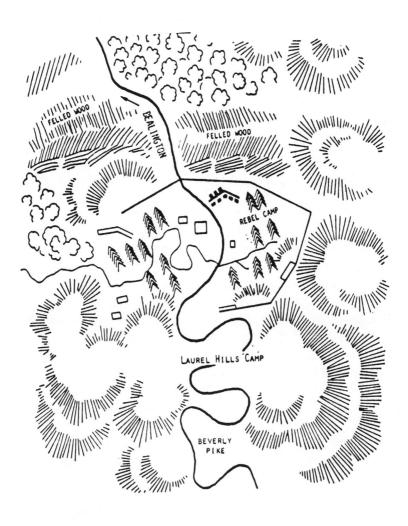

The Confederate camp at Laurel Hill, July 1861.

their victory was complete and that he possessed the enemy's former positions.

Pegram and his men spent a very difficult night stumbling through the dark wilderness in their attempt to escape capture. After about 24 hours of little rest and no food, Pegram concluded to surrender himself and those with him to the Federal troops at Beverly. Their surrender was received on the morning of the 13th by Col. Thomas W. Key of the 1st Illinois Cavalry.

Though some of Pegram's men did get away, his loss in the entire affair, including those captured at and near Rich Mountain, and those with him at Beverly, exceeded 600 men. Additionally, the Confederates suffered 33 killed and 39 wounded. The Federal loss was 12 killed and 62 wounded. [31]

General Garnett learned of Pegram's defeat during the early evening of the 11th. With Rich Mountain in enemy hands Garnett knew his flank was exposed and vulnerable. He had no option but to abandon his entrenched camp at Laurel Hill and make good his escape. Abandoning his position at midnight, Garnett and his command first marched toward Beverly, then retraced their steps toward Laurel Hill. They left the turnpike at Leadsville (Elkins), marching northward toward St. George and West Union, in an attempt to turn the mountains at the northern end of the ridges.

At dawn the next morning Union Gen. T.A. Morris quickly discovered that the Confederates had retreated in the night from Laurel Hill. After seeing that rations were issued, Morris began a relentless pursuit of Garnett's command, stopping only long enough to send a rider into Beverly for instructions from General McClellan. Resting briefly during the night Morris resumed his pursuit and at noon of the 13th skirmishing began between the Confederate rear guard and the Federal advance. When Corrick's Ford of the Cheat River was reached the Confederates attempted to establish a defensive position with driftwood and stone. Closely followed by Morris' men a fierce fight began at the river's edge and General Garnett was killed while supervising the fording of the river. Garnett's riderless horse dashed to the rear and his body was captured.

Garnett's command continued their run northward, marching all the following night to a point near West Union, when they crossed into Maryland at Red House. From there they turned southward to Greenland, Hardy County, Virginia, finally reaching Monterey after a tragic seven-day march. Monterey, a community 45 miles northwest of Staunton, soon became the scene of action for the demoralized Confederates as they attempted to refit and reorganize. On July 14, command of the Army of the Northwest passed to Gen. Henry Rootes Jackson, former governor of Georgia. General Lee and Virginia Gov. John Letcher dispatched reinforcements to Monterey and began formulating plans to regain control of

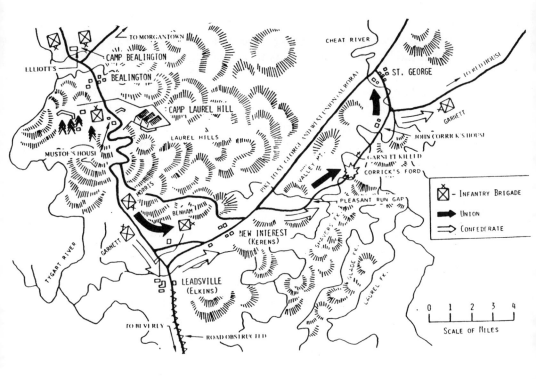

the northwest.

Pleased with his success, General McClellan issued congratulatory orders to the army on July 16: "I am more than satisfied with you. You have annihilated two armies ... You have killed more than two hundred and fifty of the enemy ... You have made long and arduous marches, often with insufficient food, frequently exposed to the inclemency of the weather .... Soldiers! I have confidence in you, and I trust you have learned to confide in me ..."[32] General McClellan's time to bask in success was cut short with the Federal defeat at Manassas, on July 21. The next day McClellan was ordered to Washington and Gen. William S. Rosecrans, hero of the battle of Rich Mountain, assumed command of the Department of the Ohio, encompassing West Virginia.

On July 23, as McClellan headed for Washington, Confederate Gen. William Wing Loring arrived at Monterey and took over command from Gen. H.R. Jackson. Loring's work would prove to be difficult indeed. He inherited an army that was defeated, demoralized, scarcely supplied and wracked with disease. So early in the conflict the men were, for the most part, still raw recruits, and many of the officers were no better trained in the business of war. It was thus truly in the face of adversity that General Loring and his subordinates would attempt to reoccupy the northwest for the Confederacy.

As the tumultuous month of July drew to a close General Lee was no doubt frustrated by the turn of events in West Virginia. In the first weeks of the conflict it is clear that Lee not only hoped, but believed, that West Virginia could be easily held for the South. His strategy of sending General Wise into the Kanawha Valley; of dispatching Maj. Francis M. Boykin to Weston and vicinity to recruit Virginia troops; of ordering Maj. Alonzo Loring to recruit at Wheeling and to destroy the rail terminal there; of ordering Col. George Portefield to Grafton before Federal troops could occupy it; all seemed to Lee and the Confederate authorities at Richmond to be sufficient to hold West Virginia. Three months into the war however, it was already apparent that their judgment was flawed. General Wise had been driven from the Kanawha Valley; General Garnett killed while retreating, his command dispersed or captured in a series of inglorious engagements with the enemy; Colonel Pegram defeated at Rich Mountain; and nearly the entire Trans-Allegheny section thus in firm Federal control. In addition, there had been skirmishes at Romney and Harpers Ferry, with Col. Thomas J. (later Stonewall) Jackson forced to abandon Harpers Ferry on June 16.[33] Also, on June 19, the Second Wheeling Convention had formed the "Restored Government of Virginia" with Francis H. Pierpont as governor. With that act Virginia now had two governments. The Confederate Government at Richmond under Gov. John Letcher, and the Restored Government at Wheeling under Pierpont. Both governments claimed authority over all of Virginia, including West Virginia. [34]

Thus we begin to understand some of the many problems facing the Confederacy in this region on the eve of General Lee's arrival from Richmond. In the first 90 days of the war the Confederates had moved westward from the Virginia Central and Virginia and Tennessee Railroads, while the U.S. forces advanced eastward along the Kanawha River, and southeastward from the line of the Baltimore and Ohio. The two forces had to overcome inclement weather, "wild" topography, snakes, bushwhackers, and their own inexperience. As the first theater of war, the early military activities in West Virginia captured the attention of the nation. General McClellan was thrust into national prominence after the victory at Rich Mountain, and many people began to realize that this conflict would not soon be terminated.

UNDER TWO FLAGS

$\mathcal{D}$uring the last half of July, Federal forces worked diligently to place a firm military grip on the areas of West Virginia under their control. With General Cox completing his occupation of the Kanawha Valley and adjacent territory, General Rosecrans concerned himself with keeping enough force in the northwest to maintain control. Some of his regiments had enlisted for three months and were now being discharged. This fact inconvenienced both Rosecrans and Cox temporarily, as the majority of those released soon returned to the field having enlisted for three years. The Reorganized Government of Virginia was functioning at Wheeling with Governor Pierpont assisting in the enlistment of "loyal" troops.

Subsequent to McClellan's departure, Rosecrans placed Gen. J.J. Reynolds in command of the Federal forces in the Tygart Valley. These men were entrenched at Cheat Mountain, Cheat Mountain Pass, Huttonsville, and Elkwater. In these positions Reynolds' men could effectively block any Confederate move westward from the direction of Staunton. Additionally, Reynolds had the potential of cutting off supplies to Confederate forces in both eastern and western Virginia. He could threaten supplies going eastward from the Shenandoah Valley by moving down the Staunton-Parkersburg Turnpike to attack the rail line at Staunton, or he could march south along the Huntersville-Huttonsville Pike to reach the Virginia Central Railroad at Millboro and eliminate supplies going to the Confederate Army in the Kanawha Valley.

The Cheat Mountain range Reynolds occupied has three distinct tops. The one known as "western top" was just that, while the second was called "middle" or "center top" or "Cheat Summit." The easternmost top had several names including "first top," "eastern ridge," and "Back Allegheny." The Federal encampment at Cheat occupied the middle top and was variously referred to as Fort Milroy, Cheat Fort, White Top and Camp McClellan. In excess of 4,000 feet in elevation, it was the highest Union encampment of the war. Situated nine miles west of Cheat Fort along the Staunton-Parkersburg Turnpike was another large camp, this one known as "Cheat Mountain Pass." Westward three miles from that position was

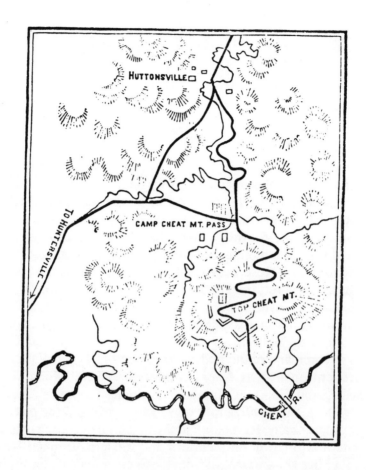

another camp in the tiny community of Huttonsville, on the Tygart's Valley River. Seven miles south of Huttonsville was "Camp Elkwater."

General Rosecrans busied himself in developing a new plan of advance and on August 3, he ordered that a special military district be formed with Gen. B.F. Kelley in command: "The line of the Baltimore and Ohio Railroad from Cumberland to Wheeling, and the Northwestern Virginia Railroad from Grafton, with the military posts, stations, and depots thereon, will, until further orders, constitute a special military district, to be called the District of Grafton ...."[1] It should be noted that the Northwestern Virginia Railroad was a branch of the B&O Railroad.

Rosecrans also ordered General Cox to construct "small field works" in the vicinity of Gauley Bridge, and he told Col. Erastus B. Tyler to occupy Summersville, Nicholas County, with his 7th Regiment Ohio Volunteer

Infantry. In that position Colonel Tyler could open a direct line of communication from the Kanawha Valley, where General Cox was, to Weston and Clarksburg, where General Rosecrans' headquarters were. Further, Rosecrans ordered scouts to patrol the region about Glenville, Gilmer County, saying it was "now infested with guerrillas." Rosecrans estimated that 10 days would be required to carry out these orders and prepare an advance on Lewisburg, Greenbrier County. He hoped to "seize Lewisburg, which is but five days' march from head of steamboat navigation on the Kanawha," and establish there "a provision depot of ample size, properly fortified." [2]

In notifying the Federal authorities at Washington of his desire to occupy Lewisburg, Rosecrans explained that once there he would prepare a "movement on Wytheville and East Tennessee." Further, he said he wanted to "seize that place, and take possession of the railroad as far down as Abingdon; break the railroad bridges down east of Wytheville, so as to prevent the enemy from coming in that direction; make a fortified depot of it and a good road from thence to the Great Falls of the Kanawha ... "[3]

Rosecrans' plans at this time seemed feasible, though in the art of warfare there are always obstacles seen and unseen. In view of the fact that the Union Army had not yet reached the principal ridge of the Alleghenies except in the vicinity of the B&O Railroad, the military situation in the

Gen. William S. Rosecrans, U.S.A.
1819-1898

Gen. J.J. Reynolds, U.S.A.
1822-1899

northwest was yet unsettled. General Reynolds' positions in the Tygart Valley were vulnerable to attack by the same routes he hoped to use in attacking the Virginia Central Railroad, and General Cox was equally open to attack in the Kanawha Valley. At Gauley Bridge the New and Gauley rivers merge to form the great Kanawha. The James River and Kanawha Turnpike paralleled New River to the east. Another road extended from Gauley Bridge to Summersville, a distance of about 30 miles, with a side road to Cross Lanes and Carnifax Ferry. From Summersville, this road continued northward to Sutton and Weston. The Giles, Fayette, and Kanawha Turnpike, extended from Kanawha Falls through Fayetteville to Flat Top Mountain, another strong position, thence to the Narrows of New River, and on to the important Virginia and Tennessee Railroad. A strong Confederate advance from the direction of the Narrows of New River, or from the direction of Lewisburg, could seriously threaten Cox's position. Additionally, General Rosecrans would soon realize that his plans of conquest would be hampered by the lack of supplies and efficient officers to lead his troops.

Less than 48 hours after notifying Washington of his planned advance Rosecrans wrote again to the authorities there complaining of the inexperience of his officers: "Every day's experience with volunteer troops convinces me of the absolute necessity of having some officers of military education among them. Whole regiments are mustered into the service and sent upon active duty without a single officer who knows thoroughly company drill, much less the organization or drill of a regiment ... " Rosecrans went on to ask that lieutenants from West Point Military Academy be sent to West Virginia as drill instructors. [4] In another dispatch that same day he was reduced to begging for help. He told the Assistant Adjutant General to ask General McClellan "for Heaven's sake, to make some such provision as I have suggested for the military instruction of the reorganized and new regiments ... " [5]

About this time Rosecrans ordered Colonel Tyler to prepare a march on Lewisburg in conjunction with General Cox. To that order "Old Rosy," as he was called, was told by Tyler that many of his men were barefoot! "The quartermaster of my regiment made requisition on post quartermaster at Clarksburg some time since for shoes, many of the men being barefooted at this time .... The rocky roads of this country make it very difficult for the men to march without shoes; many have however, been doing so for several days ... " Colonel Tyler managed to mitigate this message somewhat by informing his commander that his mere presence in Summersville had produced favorable results from the citizens: "The presence of our men ... has had a glorious effect here ... the most rabid secessionists at once embrace the Union cause, and say they have been grossly deceived by their leading men. It is a better argument in most cases than bullets. So far I find in every county we have been in a disposition ... of a large majority of the people to return to their allegiance." [6]

Developments in the northwest would further delay Rosecrans in implementing his plan. General Reynolds' men were yet engaged in fortifying their positions when the advance of some Southern forces resulted in occasional skirmishing. On August 6, Gen. Winfield Scott notified Rosecrans that they had received information that "Lee intends attacking Cheat Mountain Pass." He told Rosecrans to expedite the fortifications ordered by General McClellan. [7] The next day General McClellan sent a dispatch to Rosecrans telling him that reliable information suggested that "Lee and Johnston are actually on their march to crush you in Western Virginia. It is probable that they will move either on Huttonsville or Gauley. Complete the intrenchments .... Get your artillery in position .... Establish your own headquarters at Buckhannon...establish a telegraphic communication thence to the Gauley. In no event permit the enemy to reenter Western Virginia. Carry out these instructions immediately .... Report frequently. Push your patrols and pickets to the front ..."[8]

McClellan did not have full benefit of the facts. It was too late to prevent the Confederates from reentering West Virginia. Acting on orders from General Loring, two Confederate infantry regiments occupied the road between Huntersville and Huttonsville, as far as Valley Mountain, during the latter part of July. Their Valley Mountain camps being just 16 miles from Camp Elkwater. Also, General Loring was now encamped at Huntersville.

LORING AND LEE AT HUNTERSVILLE

*H*aving spent a few days at Monterey inspecting the troops and tending to their needs, General Loring determined to advance to Huntersville, Pocahontas County, arriving there on July 30. Loring was accompanied on his ride by his staff, Col. Carter Stevenson, assistant adjutant general; Maj. A.L. Long, chief of artillery; Capt. James L. Corley, chief quartermaster; Capt. R.G. Cole, chief commissary; Lt. H.M. Matthews, aide-de-camp, and Col. W.M. Starke, volunteer aide-de-camp. [1]

As his forces amassed in the region over the next few days, Loring soon had on the Huntersville line about 8,500 men. Additionally, there were approximately 6,000 Confederate soldiers now encamped at Bartow, on the Greenbrier River, under command of Gen. H.R. Jackson, and within easy striking distance of Cheat Mountain. Col. Stephen Lee's 6th North Carolina Infantry and Col. William Gilham's 21st Virginia Infantry, held the advance posts at and near Valley Mountain. It was these movements that had caused the Federal authorities at Washington to warn Rosecrans of an enemy advance during early August.

Loring made Huntersville his armies supply depot and headquarters, and that community very rapidly became the scene of action for the Confederates. Southern forces continued to consolidate in the area for several days, as Loring kept supply wagons running to and from Millboro, which was near the Virginia Central Railroad, southwest of Staunton. The road from Huntersville to Millboro was not well known, but it proved adequate for the movement of supplies. Just above Huntersville the road from the north split, one branch being the important route over the mountains to Millboro, the other running southward to the Kanawha Valley. Situated about 24 miles north of Warm Springs and 50 miles southwest of Monterey, Huntersville was a tiny but important community that had served for many years as a place where "merchants and tradesmen from the east would arrange to meet the hunters and barter goods." Thus the name Huntersville was given this little outpost in the wilderness. One writer recalled that "Nature seems to have marked Huntersville and vicinity as designed for something of more than ordinary importance. The

Gen. William Wing Loring,
C.S.A. 1818-1886
Courtesy Jim Raab,
St. Augustine, Fla.

locality is approachable from the four quarters of the earth by valleys converging here. The beauty of the scenery everywhere displayed is something phenomenal, in the view of all who have eyes to appreciate whatever is picturesque in mountains, forest and streams. The air is pure and exhilarating. Mineral waters abound in profusion ...." [2]

Unfortunately for soldiers of the Blue & Gray, West Virginia in the latter half of 1861 experienced unprecedented rainfall which spawned devastating disease. The natural beauty of the mountainous terrain about Huntersville and across the region proved to be in sharp contrast to the misery of typhoid, measles, dysentery, pneumonia, and other diseases which afflicted both armies without prejudice. On July 22, a cold rain began that continued for 20 successive days and intermittently for nearly eight weeks. It was under these conditions that Federal and Confederate soldiers attempted to wage war. When Loring occupied Huntersville on July 30, he found the church, courthouse, and many private homes already occupied as military hospitals, and of course this situation only grew worse as the campaigns in the area continued. One military chaplain traveling with Loring noted that Huntersville was "a wretched and filthy town." [3]

Worried about developments in the west, General Lee determined to cross the Alleghenies and supervise in person the South's West Virginia campaign. Traveling with two servants and two military aides, Col. John A. Washington and Capt. (later colonel) Walter H. Taylor, Lee left Richmond on July 28. Captain Taylor later wrote that this "journey was made as far as Staunton by rail, and from thence the party proceeded on horseback to Monterey, Highland County. The ride through the country was most enjoyable; that section abounds in lovely scenery, and the mountain air was most invigorating ... on arriving at Monterey the delights of a ride on horseback were very seriously impaired by the ... rainy season, and to the same cause is to be attributed the appalling degree of sickness that then prevailed .... " [4]

While at Staunton, Lee's party was joined by Col. Robert Hatton of the 7th Regiment Tennessee Infantry. As they prepared to leave for Monterey, Hatton wrote his wife, telling her that they would be on the way "to Millboro in a few minutes; thence to Huntersville. General Lee is here going on to take charge of the expedition .... It is reported ... that Governor Wise is retreating in this direction. We will stop him and put him to going forward again. Lee says, we will run Lincoln's men into the Ohio .... " [5]

While at Monterey General Lee held an inspection of the troops, as recalled by one member of the 37th Virginia Infantry: "Gen. Robert E. Lee, who had been assigned to West Virginia visited us and we were drawn up for dress parade. It was the first time I had ever had the pleasure of seeing General Lee. As he rode along the ranks he was so superior looking it was the unanimous opinion of the regiment he was the finest looking officer in the army. He was not then so gray as the pictures we are accustomed to ... he had an iron gray moustache instead of the full face beard. I wish I had a picture of him as he appeared that day ... " [6]

Lee and his party followed by reinforcements collected along the way continued their journey to Huntersville via Millboro and Warm Springs. On August 1, Col. Robert Hatton again wrote his wife, this time from Warm Springs: "On yesterday, my regiment moved from Millboro in direction of this place, and camped on the side of the mountain .... I was awakened by the rain falling in my face ... It rained for two and a half hours as hard as I ever saw it — perfect torrents running through our encampment, sweeping tin pans, cups, etc., into the river below .... Our road led over Warm Spring mountain ... I walked over, giving my horse to a man who carried the guns of several of the boys .... The scenery was truly sublime ... This is among the celebrated Summer resorts of Virginia ... The baths are splendid — temperature 98 Fahrenheit. The boys have been luxuriating for two hours ... " [7]

The march from Millboro to Warm Springs covered roughly 15 miles, most of which was a gradual ascent of that section of the Allegheny Mountains. Occasional periods of sunshine did not offset the fact that heavy rains had turned most of the roads in the region into little more than mudbogs, making travel exceedingly difficult. Soldiers often referred to the trails and so-called turnpikes as "hog pens" or "rivers of mud."

Another participant in the march from Millboro was Pvt. Marcus B. Toney of Tennessee. Explaining the hardships of the journey he said that after they had "trudged along some five miles in a sweltering August sun, I tried to give my six-shooter away, but could not find anyone to accept it, and over in the bushes I threw it. I then unbuckled my Damascus blade, made an offer of that, but was likewise refused, and it was thrown into the bushes. I then tried to give away a blanket, but no one would accept, so away it went. I thought, probably the war would end before the winter. By the time we reached the summit of the mountain nearly all the men in the regiment had disposed of their appendages ... Looking down from the crest of the mountain, we could see in the valley, three miles distant, the hotels and cottages of Warm Springs. The descent to the Springs was easy compared with the struggle up." [8]

With Lee and the reinforcements on the way General Loring was active at Huntersville trying to organize and supply his immediate command, while also coordinating the actions of Wise and Gen. John B. Floyd. Floyd, like Wise, was an ex-governor of Virginia. He was commissioned a Confederate general on May 23, 1861, and after the twin disaster of Garnett's defeat and Wise's retreat, he was ordered to assemble what forces he could and proceed to Jackson's River Depot to guard there the Virginia Central Railroad. [9] Floyd's commission predated that of General Wise and he was thus entitled to command their combined forces when operating together. Unfortunately, during the political campaigns of the 1850's both men developed a hatred for each other which they carried with them into the war. This fact would prove to be very detrimental to Confederate efforts in the region, and not even the persuasive and cordial Robert E. Lee would be able to ally these two political generals.

Moving toward Wise's camp near White Sulphur Springs, General Floyd received on Aug. 1, a dispatch from Loring. General Loring advised Floyd to open communication with Wise and to join him at once, if possible. Loring went on to explain that he was expecting reinforcements from Staunton, and that the enemy was encamped upon Cheat Mountain, and along the road to Beverly. "We are slowly concentrating here" he said, "for the want of transportation and supplies." Loring said he felt that if the Yankees were not "pressing in the direction of Wise," that their forces could unite in "a decided blow in the vicinity of Cheat Mountain." He asked Floyd to send him as soon as possible information of "the movements of General Wise and yourself." [10]

The next day, Aug. 2, Floyd occupied himself with attempting to obtain guns for his command. Many of the weapons his men had already been issued were found to be unsafe and nothing more than antique junk. Floyd

Gen. John B. Floyd,
C.S.A. 1806-1863

wrote that out of 28 weapons tested in one batch, "Three of the tubes were perfectly loose in the cylinder and one other blew out, breaking off the cock. Three of these guns have broken off at the breach." Despite being sent to war with arms such as these, Floyd spoiled for a fight. "My impatience to get actively into the field increases as I near the scene of action" he said, and he would soon have his chance. [11]

On Aug. 3, General Lee and his companions rode into Huntersville and went immediately to Loring's headquarters. Lee and Loring had served in the army together during the war with Mexico, at which time Loring was Lee's superior in rank. Now, by circumstances beyond their control, these two men of military prowess found themselves thrust into an "unnatural war," with Lee the ranking officer.

The two commanders discussed every aspect of the campaign underway and Loring gave Lee a dispatch from Wise dated Aug. 1. In it Wise said he was preparing his men for active campaigning and that he estimated the enemy on Gauley River to be at least 5,000 strong. Wise also said he thought the Yankees would advance slowly toward Lewisburg, and from there attack Huntersville. [12]

Lee responded immediately, telling Wise that he understood that

Wise's retreat from the Kanawha Valley had been for the purpose of uniting with General Floyd in protecting the Virginia Central Railroad. Lee asked Wise if there were any "strong positions in front of Lewisburg that you can hold, reenforced by General Floyd and the people of the country?" Explaining that it was necessary to stop the advance of the enemy east of the mountains, Lee told Wise to "halt at Lewisburg till further notice .... Send back to General Floyd to support you. Inform General Loring of the positions you will take, and be prepared by a concentration of forces to strike a blow at the enemy." [13]

Having given Wise instructions Lee wrote to General Floyd, who was then camped at Sweet Springs, Monroe County. After discussing the contents of Wise's dispatch, Lee said it was possible the Yankees might move on Lewisburg in two columns. If that were the case, Lee said he feared the enemy would "attempt to seize the Central Virginia Railroad and the Virginia and Tennessee Railroad if their force is sufficient." He told Floyd he would see "the importance of preventing this ... and of holding Lewisburg, or at least of keeping them west of the mountains." Lee closed the dispatch by ordering Floyd to "join General Wise." [14]

The following day Wise responded to Lee's dispatch, saying that he had workmen blocking the roads against an enemy advance at Bungers Ferry, west of Lewisburg, and at Big and Little Sewell Mountains, over which passed the James River and Kanawha Turnpike. He told Lee that as soon as he could refresh and refit his command he would move westward to Meadow Bluff, about one days' march from Lewisburg. From there Wise hoped to press his way back toward Gauley Bridge. Believing that Lee misunderstood his reasons for retreating from the Kanawha Valley, Wise said defense of the Virginia Central Railroad was not his main objective. He told Lee that if he had remained in the valley he would "have been shut in, cut off, or driven down through Beckley and Princeton to Wytheville." He added the complaint that "The valley was conquered by the enemy already when I got there from Charleston to Point Pleasant." Besides that, Wise said that if the Yankees had reached Lewisburg or further south that he would have been cut off from reinforcements and supplies. After briefly discussing the locations of Union troops in his area, Wise suggested that General Floyd should move his command toward Fayetteville, 12 miles from Gauley Bridge, and prepare to unite with him in attacking the enemy. "But to answer your questions," Wise said, "There are several strong positions in front of Lewisburg, which I can hold against 5,000, without ... Floyd." Adding that he believed the Yankees would reinforce Huttonsville with troops from the valley, Wise bragged that "if he does ... General Floyd and I may fall on him." [15]

After just one day in West Virginia General Lee wrote a letter to his wife, Mary Custis Lee. From this letter we can see that Lee already possessed an excellent understanding of the military situation in the west: "I reached here yesterday, dearest Mary, to visit this portion of the army ... Two regiments and a field-battery occupy the Allegheny Mountains in advance, about thirty miles ... and guards the road to Staunton. The division here guards the road leading by the Warm Springs to Millboro and Covington. Two regiments are advanced about twenty-eight miles to Middle Mountain ... South of here again is another column of our enemies ... not far from Lewisburg.... General Jackson of Georgia commands on the Monterey line, General Loring on this line, and General Wise, supported by General Floyd, on the Kanawha line .... The measles are prevalent throughout the whole army .... What a glorious world Almighty God has given us. How thankless and ungrateful we are, and how we labour to mar his gifts." [16]

The next day, Aug. 5, Lee wrote again to Wise, saying he hoped that Wise and Floyd would soon unite. Lee wondered if Floyd might be able to occupy Fayetteville, as Wise had suggested. He said also that if the army on the Huntersville line could advance over Middle and Valley Mountain's toward the Cheat Mountain range, that it would relieve pressure on the commands of Wise and Floyd. [17]

Also on Aug. 5, General Floyd issued orders from his camp at Sweet Springs for his brigade (45th and 50th Virginia Infantry) to be ready to march toward Lewisburg at five a.m. the next morning. Getting underway at the stated time Floyd's brigade marched to within two miles of Wise's camp at White Sulphur Springs. That evening Floyd went in person to confer with Wise. Their meeting was not a cordial one and when Floyd learned that Lee had not given Wise any specific orders, he said he would prepare to immediately occupy Lewisburg and then mount an attack against the enemy on the Gauley River. Of course Wise protested the move, saying that he would require at least 10 days to refit his command with clothing and acquire enough wagons for an advance. In the face of Wise's opposition Floyd gave him no orders to accompany his brigade, but remained adamant that an advance would be made. [18]

Unwilling to surrender the issue without a fight, Wise wrote to Lee early the next morning complaining of Floyd's perceived obstinate attitude. This had been the two ex-governors first conference of the war, and it was already obvious there would be no cooperation between them. Wise wasted no time in asking Lee to issue an order separating his command from that of General Floyd. "Please assign to each one respective fields of operation," Wise asked, adding that he thought Floyd's Brigade should guard the Fayetteville and Beckley roads, while his Legion guarded the road into Lewisburg. [19]

With General Loring busy coordinating the movements of their various commands, reinforcements continued to pour into Huntersville and

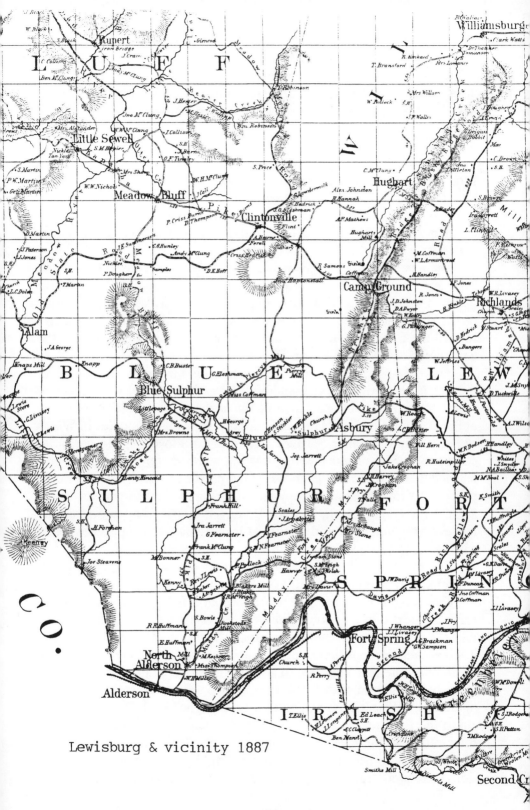

Lewisburg & vicinity 1887

-34-

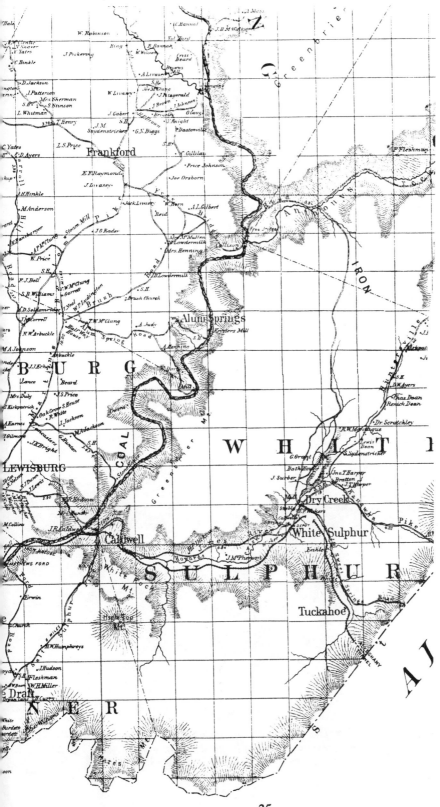

vicinity. Numerous pastures and gently sloping hillsides of the area were converted into military camps, and the white tents of hungry, tired soldiers dotted the roadsides for miles around. The army hospitals continued their seemingly endless work, and so many men became ill during this time that R.T. Coleman, regimental surgeon of the 21st Virginia Infantry, referred to the area around Huntersville as "the Valley of the Shadow of Death." Surgeon Coleman was not exaggerating the case. Another member of his regiment, George Peterkin, wrote after the war that 600 of 900 men in the 21st Virginia were hospitalized during the month of August. [20]

Among the young Southern boys marching into the face of despair was Pvt. Sam Watkins of the 1st Tennessee Infantry. Watkins wrote of Huntersville that it was "a little but sprightly town hid in the very fastnesses of the mountains." He said the local inhabitants lived very well in the mountains, and that they "had plenty of honey and buckwheat cakes," and that "Everything seemed to grow in the mountains—potatoes, Irish and sweet; onions, snap beans, peas—though the country was very thinly populated." Watkins said that wild game was abundant as were apples

Marlinton, W.Va. in 1899. This community was known as Marling's Bottom during the war years and was the site of frequent military activity.
Courtesy Pocahontas County Historical Society, via Bill McNeel

PRESBYTERIAN CHURCH
...
The Huntersville Presbyterian
Church of colonial style with
balcony for slaves was built,
1854, and used by all denomi-
nations. Used as hospital and
garrison for Confederate and
Union troops. Masonic Hall
added, 1896, as second story.

WEST VIRGINIA HISTORIC COMMISSION, 1963

1991 view inside the Huntersville church. Courtesy Larry Taylor, Minnehaha Springs, W.Va.

Above: Huntersville, W.Va., in 1888. Below: The former Pocahontas County Courthouse at Huntersville, W.Va., about 1899. In 1893, the county seat was moved to Marlinton. Photos courtesy Pocahontas County Historical Society, via Bill McNeel.

and peaches, and "everywhere the people had apple-butter." [21]

Huntersville at this time was rapidly being transformed from a trading center and small county capitol, into one of the most active military depots in the region. This fact did not meet the approval of some citizens, although the majority of Pocahontas County residents were Southern in sympathy. The facts of life were such that with the arrival of troops there came necessarily a loss of personal liberty and privacy. Whether their homes were located behind Federal or Confederate lines, civilians discovered that they could no longer move freely along the public roads nor could they expect the soldiers to stay out of their churches, schools, places of business and homes.

On Aug. 6, General Lee rode out of Huntersville on his way to the front lines at Valley Mountain, some 28 miles distant. Having determined that a few more days would be required before the bulk of Loring's men could advance into the Tygart Valley, Lee decided to join the two regiments already at the front. Once established in camp on Valley Mountain, Lee received the dispatch from General Wise in which he asked to have his command separated from that of his rival General Floyd. Poor Wise was not to have his way. Lee told him that to "assign to each respective fields of action ... would be contrary to the purpose of the President ... and destroy the prospect of success." [22]

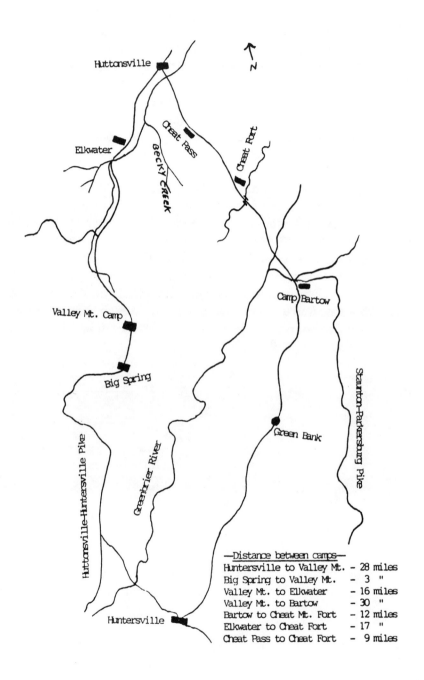

Huttonsville

N

Cheat Pass

Cheat Fort

Elkwater

BECKY CREEK

Camp Bartow

Valley Mt. Camp

Big Spring

Green Bank

Huttonsville-Huntersville Pike

Greenbrier River

Staunton-Parkersburg Pike

Huntersville

—Distance between camps—
Huntersville to Valley Mt. – 28 miles
Big Spring to Valley Mt.   –   3   "
Valley Mt. to Elkwater   – 16 miles
Valley Mt. to Bartow   – 30   "
Bartow to Cheat Mt. Fort   – 12 miles
Elkwater to Cheat Fort   – 17   "
Cheat Pass to Cheat Fort   –   9 miles

THE INVISIBLE ENEMY

*W*hen Robert E. Lee arrived at Valley Mountain on the evening of Aug. 6, he joined there the 21st Virginia and 6th North Carolina Infantry regiment's. Lee's arrival upon this rugged and foreboding mountain so near the enemy camps was an event long remembered by many of those who witnessed it: "General Robert E. Lee, having been assigned to the command of this department, joined us here and pitched his tent about one or two hundred yards from our company. He soon won the affection of all by his politeness and notice of the soldiers. He very often had something to say to the men; and it soon became known that when some of the people in the neighborhood sent him something good to eat, the articles were sent to some sick soldier as soon as the messenger got out of sight..." [1]

Also writing of Lee's arrival on the mountain, a member of the 6th North Carolina Infantry recalled the positive result of their commanders presence: "Our courage, already full and determined, breathed a new life, for we saw in him a leader in whom were met and blended those elements that would illustrate all that was meant by 'our cause and strife.' His person was the finest we had ever seen. There was only a bold hint of silver in his hair. His eye, lustrous and clear as a mountain brooklet, seemed in its normal line of vision never to fall below the distant horizon, and yet our souls were pierced by the mingled pathos and nobility of his look ... " [2]

General Lee had been accompanied on his ride from Huntersville not only by his staff, but also by a battalion of Virginia cavalry commanded by his 24 year old son, Maj. William Henry Fitzhugh Lee. Referred to as "Rooney" to distinguish him from his first cousin, Maj. (later Gen.) Fitzhugh Lee was Harvard educated and had served in the U.S. Army from 1857 to 1859. We see from a letter written by another Confederate officer that Fitzhugh, like his father, occasionally made a strong impression on those around him: "Gen. Lee has a son encamped with our Brigade. He is Major of Cavalry. A fine looking, and spirited man. Looks nearly as old as his father. Not so fine looking as his father, however. Has spent part of today at my tent. Is highly educated; full of Virginia pride—a Virginian in manner, and bearing. Gen. Lee is, you know, the son of 'Lightfoot Harry

Lee,' Washington's pet, in the Revolution. His family, therefore, is of royal extraction, and hence, my particularity in references to him. Characters of historic interest. The mother of this Major, was the granddaughter of Mrs. George Washington." [3]

Once established at Valley Mountain General Lee did not delay informing himself, by personal reconnaissance and with the aid of scouts, of the condition of affairs in the Federal Army to his front. Lee also endeavored to familiarize himself with the topographic conditions of the immediate field of action; at the same time taking general oversight of operations on the Kanawha line by frequent correspondence with Generals Wise and Floyd. Lee found himself facing an enemy of unknown strength in a region of dense wilderness and truly burdensome terrain. Human habitations were few and far between and those that did exist were usually crude, hardscrabble dwellings. Another problem was the fact that some local inhabitants were Union in sympathy, and those families were sometimes the source of anti-Confederate bushwhackers. In this area of Virginia however, that particular breed of mountaineer was more frequently a menace to the boys in blue.

The heavy rains that had fallen now for nearly three weeks were joined in their fury by unseasonably cold temperatures. The Federal forces occupying the top of Cheat Mountain found themselves snow covered from time to time, and Blue & Gray troops encamped at lower elevations were alternately subjected to snow or heavy frost. All this in the "mild" month of August. Of course the invisible enemy, disease, flourished, as hundreds of men on both sides of the issue suffered and died an early death.

In their camp near the top of Allegheny Mountain, 10 miles above Monterey, the sad experience of the 3rd Arkansas Infantry exemplified that of most other soldiers in West Virginia in 1861. Under the immediate command of Gen. H.R. Jackson and functioning as a "right wing" to Loring's command at Huntersville, the Arkansas men had only been in camp two weeks when a near epidemic of measles broke out. Their campsite became a miserable and sodden field of mud, which the troops dubbed "Camp Measles." [4]

On Aug. 8, Capt. George Alexander of Company I, 3rd Arkansas Infantry, wrote to the parents of Pvt. William Prior, of Tulip, Arkansas, to inform them of their only son's death: "It becomes my painful duty to inform you of the death of your son William, who died the night of the sixth, of measles and mumps combined. He was delirious all day and died insensible. On the Sunday previous Lt. Taylor was sent to see our sick ... over 150 ... He found your son very sick and had prayer in his tent, and left him with no idea of his being dangerous .... I can truly say ... I had no better soldier in my company....Lt. Taylor, on his return last night, reported that he took the body ... to Monterey .... He was buried by the side of the other soldiers, on a beautiful knoll, in a lovely meadow ... " [5] (William Prior was 18 years old.)

Another member of the 3rd Arkansas wrote to his parents of their hardships and loneliness: "Last night was Sunday night, a night always commemorated by you all by singing the sacred melodies which have been hymned in our house since childhood. Billy Paisley, Dunkan Durkam, Mr. Jones, and myself gathered around one of our camp fires and made the camp ring with some of the same good old songs which we have learned to love for their very age ... I remembered you all then, and imagination showed me the lighted parlor, and my ear caught the sound of my mother's voice as she sang the treble to some of those time honored songs, and my heart ran out in sighs that I might be permitted once again to be with you all at home, dear home." [6]

Adequate records of the extent to which disease played a role in the Confederacy's defeat in West Virginia do not exist. Such records do exist however for the Federal forces and the facts which they reveal are formidable and tragic. It has been estimated that at the time General Lee occupied Valley Mountain that General Reynolds' Union troops in the area had already been reduced one-half, from 8,000 to 4,000 by disease. The majority of those soldiers were only temporarily removed from duty, but nevertheless the staggering size of the problem was an insurmountable obstacle to any offensive campaign.

The reported cases of disease in the entire Federal Department of West Virginia for the period July to October 1861, was 20,279. During this same period the numbers of Union troops in West Virginia ranged from approximately 10,000 to 25,000. With such a high disease rate among so few soldiers it is obvious that many of these men were repeatedly sick and unavailable for duty. When the time frame for these statistics is expanded to include the last two months of 1861 the facts are even more alarming. In the Union Army there were reported over this period 1,101 cases of measles, 2,089 cases of typhoid fever, 2,569 cases of malaria, 2,026 cases of other types of fever, 1,656 cases of rheumatism, and numerous other ailments and injuries which the available records do not reflect. Further, it is safe to assume that all of these statistics were worse among the Southerners, who were generally less well-supplied and who were also unaccustomed to the weather in this region.

Had medical science and proper camp sanitation been advanced further than it was in 1861 much of the disease problem would have been reduced. Most of the regimental surgeons and commanders in both armies were inexperienced in field sanitation. They did not realize, for example, that hilly terrain contributed to the drainage of surface water and human excrement from camps into water supplies at lower levels. Also to be considered is the fact that all of the regiments involved were new. The men had not yet built up their stamina and ability to endure such hardships. Hospital facilities, segregation, and medical supply were poor. Insufficient accommodations for the sick, inadequate nursing, bad food and cold, wet weather, all contributed to the end result. [7]

Writing after the war, General Lee's aide and confidant, Col. Walter H. Taylor, described the situation in West Virginia: "The season was a most unfavorable one: for weeks it rained daily and in torrents; the condition of the roads was frightful; they were barely passable. It was very seriously debated whether the army could be fed where it was ... Time and time again could be seen double teams of horses struggling with six or eight barrels of flour, and the axle of the wagon scraping and leveling the road-bed; in other words, the wagons were hub-deep in mud, and could only be moved step by step ... measles and a malignant type of fever ... prostrated hundreds ... In the subsequent campaigns of the Army of Northern Virginia the troops were subjected to great privations and to many very severe trials ... but never did I experience the same heart-sinking emotions as when contemplating the wan faces and the emaciated forms of those hungry, sickly, shivering men of the army at Valley Mountain!" [8]

Col. Walter H. Taylor, Lee's aide and personal friend, as photographed on April 1, 1861, when Taylor was 1st Lieutenant of Co. F. 6th Va. Militia.
Courtesy Carroll Walker and Janet Taylor, Norfolk, Va.

General Lee and "Traveller," a horse he purchased in 1862 after first borrowing it during the West Virginia campaign of 1861. Courtesy Washington & Lee University

BLOOD ON THE LAUREL

From his tent on Valley Mountain Lee wrote to his wife on Aug. 9: "I have been here, dear Mary, three days, coming from Monterey to Huntersville and thence here. We are on the dividing ridge looking north down the Tygart's river valley ... north of us lie Huttonsville and Beverly, occupied by our invaders, and the Rich Mountains west, the scene of our former disaster, and the Cheat Mountains east, their present stronghold .... It has rained, I believe, some portion of every day since I left Staunton .... Colonel Washington, Captain Taylor, and myself are in one tent ... I have enjoyed the company of Fitzhugh since I have been here .... I find that our old friend, J. J. Reynolds, of West Point memory, is in command of the troops immediately in front of us .... I think we shall shut up this road to the Central Railroad which they strongly threaten. Our supplies come up slowly. The men are suffering from the measles, etc ... " [1]

When Lee mentioned to Mary that their old friend General Reynolds commanded the army at his front, he could not have known the extent to which Reynolds had prepared, and continued to prepare, for any offensive Lee might launch. Writing home to the *Indianapolis Journal* from his camp at Huttonsville, a cavalryman with "Brackens Rangers" described the Federal positions: "This town is about twelve miles south-east of Beverly...At this post we have General Reynold's headquarters, the 13th Indiana regiment, half of the 3rd Ohio regiment, half of the Bracken Rangers, and one battery of four guns ... all of them captured at Rich Mountain. Twelve miles ... south-easterly brings the solitary horseman to the top of Cheat Mountain, and also to the 14th Indiana regiment ... the other half of the cavalry and a battery of four guns .... south six miles the 15th Indiana regiment, half of the 3rd Ohio, and a battery of six guns are located .... our force at the three camps ... something over 4,000, and with the troops at Beverly and those on the way here from Clarksburg, will make quite a little squad .... One or two skirmishes have taken place ... Our loss has been one horse killed, one man slightly wounded, and another's hurt mortally." [2]

Another correspondent of the same newspaper described the chaplain of the 15th Regiment Indiana Infantry: "The 15th Indiana has a regular brick of a chaplain—I forget his name ... He carries a short sword, a sword cane and three revolvers. I don't know whether he has a Testament or not."[3] And a few days later yet another letter: "There are now stationed at Cheat Mountain Pass the 13th and 17th Indiana regiments ... and on a hill ten miles east, and protected by strong fortifications, the 14th Indiana and 24th and 25th Ohio regiments." [4]

Strong earthworks and fortifications were built at each Federal camp-site and no effort was spared in defensive preparations. The strongest of the camps was Fort Milroy atop Cheat Mountain. This fort was built where the turnpike made an abrupt descent on both sides. Hundreds of pine trees were felled with the branches partially cut off and the trees placed around the camp, with the points out. Inside the felled timber strong walls of log were constructed and a deep ditch dug. Breastworks spanned the road on either side and were furnished with cannon, which on the east side had the ability to sweep the approach to the fort to the distance of one mile. At Camp Elkwater an extensive fortification was thrown across the Tygart Valley, outside of which was a trench six feet deep and 14 feet wide. The valley at this point is about 300 yards wide and at either end of the earthwork were cannons ranging diagonally across the valley. [5]

Col. Elijah Cavins commanded the 14th Regiment Indiana Infantry and personally supervised the construction of Fort Milroy at Cheat summit. He described their camp in a letter to his wife: "We are building large fortifications at this point. We will have this place so fortified in two weeks, that it will require more than 4 men to one to take it. We will have a fort, and between one and two miles of breastwork—besides the trees are cut down, over which it is impossible for an enemy to pass ... in force ... Our pickets within a quarter of a mile of our camp often get scared at night and think they see the Rebels. Night before last a panic came over some of the pickets, and four of them shot, and the whole camp were called to arms .... A number of our officers have resigned ... " [6]

The inclement weather precluded any effective military operations during this time and both armies contented themselves in scouting and fortifying. There was a severe lack of provisions in the armies due to the poor state of the roads, with the Confederates getting the worst of the deal, being the furthest from their supply base and seldom having on hand more than a two day supply of food.

On Aug. 12, General Loring arrived at Valley Mountain having successfully established a line of supply into the Tygart Valley from Monterey. Lee briefed Loring on the situation and told him of what he had learned through personal reconnaissance of the countryside to their front and flanks. It was about this time that Lee began to seriously consider an attack against the Yankees at Cheat summit. With a break in the rains and the discovery of a wilderness route by which the fort could be reached, Lee reasoned that it would be possible to dislodge Reynolds' army.

Of course the Yankees were aware that such an attempt might be made, they just didn't know when or by what route. General Rosecrans was active from his headquarters in Clarksburg coordinating the actions of Generals Reynolds and Cox, while at the same time advising McClellan of developments. West Virginia seemed to be one giant rumor mill in 1861, and in the northwest the growing rumors of Federal defeat caused a near panic among some representatives of the "Restored Government" at Wheeling under Francis Pierpont. New-state Sen. John S. Carlile grew so concerned that he telegraphed the following message to the authorities in Washington, D. C., on Aug. 15, 1861: "Lee has one body of 8,000 men near Monterey, in Highland; another force of equal if not greater strength is this side of Huntersville. Still another body of considerable size is marching by the way of Mingo Flats on to Huttonsville. We have no force guarding the Mingo Flats road. Rosecrans is at Clarksburg, a respectful distance. For God's sake send us more troops and a general to command, or else we are whipped in less than ten days. The Huntersville force and Wise and Floyd's force are all moving on us by the way of Mingo Flats, and we are without any guard or fortifications to that pass."[7]

Carlile's almost hysterical exclamation, "For God's sake send us more troops ... or we are whipped .... " was made based on nothing more than rumor and fear. There was no way for Senator Carlile or anyone at Wheeling to better grasp the military situation than the commanders in the field, among whom there was no evidence of panic. The senator's telegram passed to General McClellan from Simon Cameron, President Lincoln's Secretary of War. Apparently accepting Carlile's version of military affairs in the west, McClellan fired-off an angry and scolding telegram to General Rosecrans at Clarksburg: "I have learned from the most reliable authority that Cheat Mountain Pass was not fortified as I directed ... Carry out my previous instructions to the fullest extent .... Occupy Kanawha Valley with the minimum force necessary ... Secure Grafton and the railroad ... Disregard, for the present, the interior of Western Virginia, or else hold it with your worst troops...Concentrate in the vicinity of Huttonsville ... Strengthen fortifications as rapidly as possible, and take there all your available artillery. Make a ... reconnaissance ... of the enemy's works towards Huntersville, and if possible drive them out ... Communicate this at once by telegraph to Reynolds." [8]

Senator Carlile overacted out of ignorance and General McClellan overacted out of political concern. The Cheat Pass was well fortified days before Carlile's letter and Wise and Floyd were no where near the Tygart Valley, nor would they ever be. McClellan had personally secured the area around Grafton and the railroad before he left West Virginia on July 23. He knew that of course, and it must have been for the senator's benefit that

THE SECESSIONIST ARMY—IRREGULAR RIFLEMEN OF THE ALLEGHANIES, VIRGINIA.

he issued a redundant order.

Attempting to further pacify both McClellan and the West Virginia politicians, General Rosecrans issued a proclamation to the "Loyal Citizens of Western Virginia" on Aug. 20: "... you have a right to stand in the position you have assumed, faithful to the constitution and laws of Virginia as they were before the ordinance of secession. The Confederates...contrary to your interest and your wishes... have brought war on your soil. Their tools and dupes told you you must vote for secession...that unless you did so, hordes of abolitionists would overrun you, plunder your property, steal your slaves, abuse your wives and daughters, seize upon your lands, and hang all who opposed them...Eastern Virginians who have been accustomed to rule you...have conspired to tie you to the desperate fortunes of the Confederacy or drive you from your homes...put an end to the savage war waged by individuals who...lurk in the bushes and waylay messengers or shoot sentries, I shall be obliged to hold the neighborhood in which these outrages are committed responsible.... Citizens of Western Virginia, your fate is mainly in your own hands....If you stand firm for law and order...you may dwell together peacefully and happily as in former days."[9]

On the same date that Rosecrans issued his proclamation the Second Wheeling Convention for the Restored Government of Virginia was coming to a close. After much acrimonious debate, the convention agreed upon a new state with 39 counties, all west of the Allegheny Mountains. This was to be called the state of Kanawha.

General Lee and his Confederates at this time had a different kind of politics with which to contend. Matters were heating up near the Kanawha Valley between Wise and Floyd. On Aug. 11, General Floyd assumed command of all Southern forces intended to operate against the Yankees in the Kanawha Valley and vicinity.[10] This order did not set well with General Wise and he made no secret of it. On Aug. 13, Wise repeated his request to Lee that his command be separated from Floyd's. General Lee denied the request, citing the military situation. [11]

On Aug. 14, Lee wrote to General Floyd, acknowledging his decision to assume command of the troops on the Kanawha line, and saying that he hoped Floyd could cooperate with Wise and the local militia to drive back the invaders. Lee said he believed Floyd should be able to make a "material diversion...on the enemy's right, and while threatening his center a successful attack may be made on his left." Lee explained that his movements on the Huntersville line had caused the Yankees to draw reinforcements from Sutton and Summersville, which he thought would lessen pressure on the Army of the Kanawha. Lee said the "constant rains...have rendered the roads almost impassable, which has paralyzed operations in this quarter for the present. I have thought it probable that the extension of the enemy's force was intended to influence the elections in favor of the Pierpont government." General Floyd had earlier requested that he be sent some additional cavalry. Lee said he had none to spare, and concluded by telling Floyd that General Wise "will join you as soon as possible...and give the most hearty and zealous cooperation in repulsing the enemy." [12]

Within the next few days Wise and Floyd advanced along the James River and Kanawha Turnpike into Fayette County. In a series of brief skirmishes with Federal scouts at Big Sewell Mountain and Hawks Nest they encamped on Aug. 20, less than 10 miles from the troops of General Cox at and near Gauley Bridge. Even in such close proximity to the enemy these two political generals could not get along well enough to camp together. Wise's camp was situated along the turnpike east of Hawks Nest (present day Hawks Nest State Park), and Floyd camped a few miles away along a side road which led into Nicholas County via Carnifax Ferry.

On the night of Aug. 21, Floyd crossed the Gauley River at Carnifax Ferry. Once on the north bluffs overlooking the Gauley River, in a horseshoe-shaped bend of the river, Floyd began to entrench, designating his location as Camp Gauley.[13] The next morning he wrote to Lee informing him of his activities and asking for three regiments to replace the Wise Legion.[14] On Aug. 24, General Wise wrote to Lee from his position near Hawks Nest, complaining yet again about Floyd's attempts to merge their commands, and asking once more that they be separated.[15] Lee replied immediately: "The Army of the Kanawha is too small for active and successful operations to be divided at present. I beg, therefore, for the sake of the cause you have so much at heart, you will permit no division of sentiment or action to disturb its harmony or arrest its efficiency."[16] One can almost feel Lee's exasperation in attempting to pacify the old governor!

The following day 175 men of Floyd's cavalry left Camp Gauley and rode through Wise's camp near Hawks Nest. Advancing westward along the turnpike in a careless fashion, Floyd's men were ambushed by members of the 11th Ohio Infantry who were hiding in the woods along the road. Chaos prevailed and after the smoke cleared the Confederates had suffered an embarrassing defeat, having 16 wounded and one killed. [17]

The fortunes of war seemed to smile on General Floyd however, as the next day, Aug. 26, his men surprised and thoroughly routed the 7th Regiment Ohio Infantry at Cross Lanes, Nicholas County. Col. Erastus B. Tyler commanded the 7th Ohio and even though he was encamped within a few miles of the Confederates at Camp Gauley, he failed to post sufficient pickets or properly scout the area. Attacked just after dawn of the 26th, and outnumbered nearly three to one, Tyler's men fought well but were soon overcome and routed. The Federal loss was at least two killed, 29 wounded, and 110 captured. Floyd's losses were comparatively light with a few killed and wounded.[18]

Needless to say, General Floyd hailed this as a great victory, and General Wise was jealous! The Yankee's had been eating breakfast when attacked and Wise thus referred to the fight as the "Battle of Knives and Forks." General Floyd maintained his position above Carnifax Ferry and Wise held the turnpike east of Hawks Nest with 1,436 men.[19] Floyd's command at this time numbered approximately 2,000. Also potentially available in the area were 2,100 men of the 19th and 27th Brigade's Virginia militia, commanded by Gen. Alfred Beckley and Gen. A.A. Chapman, respectively.

On Aug. 27, Floyd sent General Lee word of his victory at Cross Lanes: "They were posted about three miles from my camp in a commanding position, but our men made the attack with spirit and soon carried it....The result of this fight will enable me to hold this quarter of the country, I think, and to cut off communication between General Cox and the forces toward the north....Amongst the killed is a captain....We captured some of their wagons and hospital supplies..." [20]

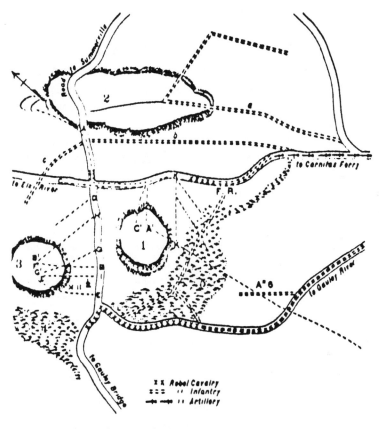

BATTLEFIELD OF CROSS LANES, VA.

August 26th, 1861

Floyd's victory did indeed enable him to temporarily cut off Federal communication between Gauley Bridge and Clarksburg. When word of Tyler's defeat reached McClellan he was furious. He ordered General Rosecrans to proceed south from Clarksburg and attack Floyd. This movement by Rosecrans into Nicholas County set the stage for the battle of Carnifax Ferry in September.

General Lee congratulated Floyd on Aug. 31: "I take great pleasure in congratulating you on the dispersion of the forces of General Tyler and the handsome victory gained by a portion of your command....A movement of the troops south of New River to a favorable point on the Kanawha will cause the retirement of General Cox from Gauley Bridge and enable you to unite your troops for an effective blow." [21]

With these events the month of August passed into history. The Confederate Government had accomplished little in West Virginia, and just four months into the war it seemed that division of the Old Dominion was assured. The Southern press began very early complaining about Lee's failure to quickly win West Virginia for the Confederacy. Before Lee had any realistic opportunity to succeed in the west, some in the press dubbed him "Granny Lee" and began to question his competence. Little did they know that with the perspective of a few years Lee would become deiform in the annals of military history.

To Carnifax Ferry

*A*ttention remained focused on the Kanawha line as inaccurate scouting reports caused General Floyd to believe that the Yankees were moving on his camp from Gauley Bridge. Floyd advised General Wise of the reports and suggested he occupy Gauley Bridge as soon as General Cox's men abandoned it. Wise found the reports incredulous but at 4 a.m. of Sept. 1 he received another dispatch from Floyd saying that a large body of the enemy were then just 12 miles from his camp. He told Wise to reinforce him with the majority of his command, leaving a small detachment to guard the turnpike and side road by which the Yankees might fall on the rear of his position. Surprisingly enough Wise complied with this order and marched about three miles down the Sunday Road to the cliffs of Gauley River opposite Floyd's encampment. At that time General Floyd received a new report stating that the entire affair was a false alarm. He then sent Wise instructions to return to his former position, which he did, but later complained that he was "disgusted by these vacillating and harassing orders." [1]

Believing he could draw the Yankees in closer to Gauley Bridge and relieve pressure on Floyd's position, General Wise used his Legion and the local militia to attack the enemy on Sept. 2 and 3. These attacks were carried out in the vicinity of Gauley Bridge and did succeed in causing General Cox to draw troops in from some of their outlying positions. The Federals suffered a total of six men wounded and three captured in the combined attacks. Confederate losses were 11 men killed and wounded.[2]

General Wise put the best possible face on the attacks in his report to General Lee, and at the same time General Floyd issued a proclamation addressed "To all whom it may concern." Floyd was disturbed with the fact that his occupation of the area had caused some people to abandon their homes. In his statement to the public Floyd said he had come into western Virginia to vindicate the political supremacy of the State. He said no one who had cast a vote for the Union would be harassed as long as they did not openly oppose the Confederacy. On the other hand, Floyd said that anyone who aided or abetted the "murderous invaders" of Virginia would be arrested for treason. [3]

On Sept. 4, the day after Floyd's proclamation, General Lee received from the authorities at Richmond permission to return to that city "Whenever, in your judgment, circumstances will justify it..." Lee had gone west at his own suggestion and Confederate President Jefferson Davis had not "ceased to feel an anxious desire" for his return. [4]

Also on the 4th General Lee wrote to Floyd saying that his men needed salt and could not get any. Lee asked whether or not a supply could be procured in the Kanawha Valley and sent to him, and he also complained that it was "impossible to obtain reliable information of the strength of the enemy in our front." Unfortunately for the boys in gray it was equally impossible for the Army of the Kanawha to reach the Kanawha Salines, near Charleston, and obtain salt. [5]

General Rosecrans was also active over this period. Pursuant to General McClellan's orders after the fiasco at Cross Lanes, Rosecrans moved south from Clarksburg with 5,000 soldiers to attack Floyd. At Sutton on Sept. 6, he issued orders for his troops to "move tomorrow morning in the direction of Summersville."[6]

Advancing in good time Rosecrans' men reached the Big Birch River just north of Summersville on Sept. 8. That afternoon he wrote to Cox at Gauley Bridge giving their position and saying that they would move on Summersville the next day. Rosecrans added that his men were "endeavoring to conceal our movements to the latest period." He also asked Cox if he could launch a diversionary attack on the Confederates the next day, so as to draw their attention away from Summersville.[7]

General Floyd's scouts reported the approach of the enemy column and at 1 a.m. of Sept. 9 Floyd notified Wise that an attack was imminent. He told Wise to send back a regiment of infantry which he had borrowed and also to send one of his own. [8] Receiving the order at 8:30 a.m. Wise neglected to answer immediately. Instead he wrote to General Lee at 10:00 a.m. complaining in his childish way that he was again "harassed with orders which I find it difficult...to comply with." Wise said that he and Floyd were camped three miles apart and that Floyd was reinforced "to the number of about 3,000 men" (actually just 1,900). In a remarkable display of either ignorance or deceit Wise told General Lee that he did not believe the reports that 6,000 Yankees were about to attack his rival at Camp Gauley. He also took the opportunity to complain about a dispute he was having with Floyd over an artillery piece at White Sulphur Springs. Both generals had been expecting the arrival of some new artillery and one of Wise's men took possession of a rifled cannon which Floyd claimed was intended for him! Floyd issued arrest orders for the man and Wise declared that he would "dispatch counter orders to those of General Floyd." [9]

Adding incompetence to insolence General Floyd also wrote to Lee on

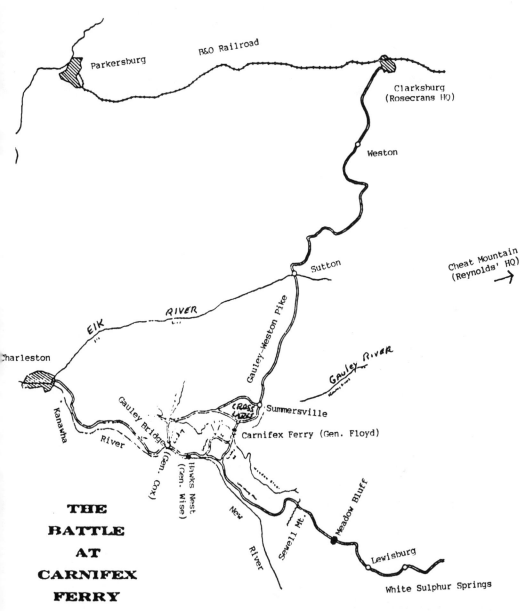

THE
BATTLE
AT
CARNIFEX
FERRY

Courtesy of W. Va. **Department of Natural Resources**

the 9th in an odd display of bravado. Despite the fact that a numerically superior army was about to offer their greetings, Floyd declared that after observing the region he was "satisfied...that the enemy must be driven out." (No kidding.) Further, he told Lee that it was "quite attainable to cross the Ohio River and lay waste the right bank of the river, so as to force a withdrawal of the enemy from Virginia..." [(10)]

At 4 p.m. of Sept. 9 Wise replied to Floyd's order for reinforcements. He said he had sent back the infantry regiment which belonged to Floyd anyway, but that he would not send a regiment of his own. Arguing that it was best to leave his Legion were it was, Wise said that even with assistance from the militia he was in danger of being overwhelmed by the enemy. In truth there was some validity to Wise's statement, because he was in a position to prevent the enemy from attacking Floyd's left flank. Had he moved his entire command to Camp Gauley the Yankees could have attacked by front and flank simultaneously. [11]

The next morning, Sept. 10, Wise wrote again to General Floyd at 6:30 a.m. In this dispatch, Wise explained in additional detail why he should not reinforce Floyd with his Legion. He stated that he believed Camp Gauley should be abandoned and Floyd's forces used along with the militia to secure the area his men now held. Wise hoped to take his command "over New River to Coal River, to penetrate Kanawha Valley whenever I can strike a blow below the falls, or Charleston, even, and to protect our loyal citizens in Boone, Cabell, and Kanawha Counties..." Neither of these two political generals would have the opportunity to implement their bold (if not ignorant) plans of conquest. General Rosecrans and company had other plans which were about to reach fruition. [12]

The Confederate defensive line at Camp Gauley was designed in the shape of a horseshoe, with an earthen redoubt located at the front of the camp. The redoubt was about 312 feet long and included a parapet battery, 350 feet in front and center, from which the Southern artillery had been positioned so as to fire over the parapet. A trench protected the battery epaulement. On both sides of the redoubt had been constructed high fences of wooden stakes, known as palisades. Log breastworks, used to screen the exterior slopes of the camp, were in a direct line with the front and curves of the defensive line. The left flank, which included more open ground than the right, was some 4,359 feet in length and had a double line of breast-works for added protection. The right flank was about equal length to the left, and was more easily defended due to the slope directly in advance of it. Both flanks, as well as the majority of the battlefield, were covered with dense forest growth, a heavy undergrowth of Laurel thickets, ravines, and rocky terrain. The road to the ferry led directly up the earthen redoubt over a natural glacis.

Early in the afternoon of Sept. 10, Gen. Henry Benham, acting on Rosecrans' orders, advanced nearer the position believed held by Floyd's army. Benham's force consisted of the 10th Regiment Ohio Infantry. As the Ohioans advanced cautiously at about 3:15 p.m., the entire Confederate line, artillery included, opened fire.

General Benham quickly sent word to his commander that reinforcements were needed. Being so far in the advance it took almost one hour

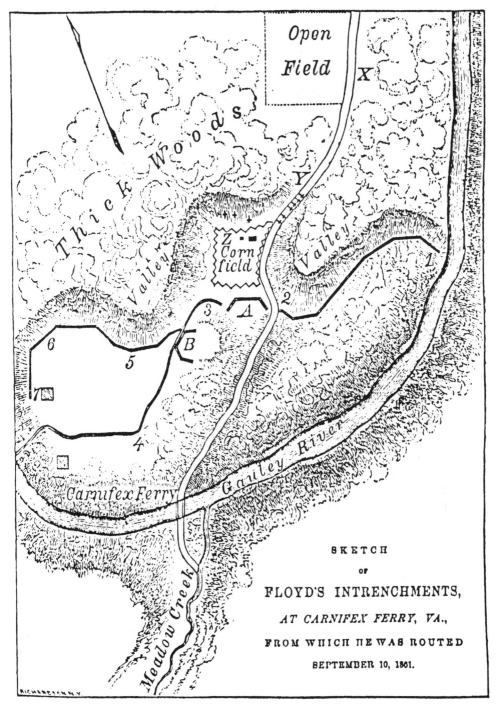

Open Field

X

Thick Woods

Y

Valley

Z Corn field

Valley

1

3 A

2

B

6

5

7

4

Gauley River

Carnifex Ferry

Meadow Creek

SKETCH
OF
FLOYD'S INTRENCHMENTS,
AT CARNIFEX FERRY, VA.,
FROM WHICH HE WAS ROUTED
SEPTEMBER 10, 1861.

1, 2, 3, 4, Inner Rebel Line.

5, 6, 7, Outer "   "   " on crest of hill, protecting rebel right flank.

A B, Rebel batteries.

A, Rebel main battery, commanding the road.

X Y, Road to Carnifex Ferry.

V, First position of our guns, consisting of two rifled 6-pounders and four mountain howitzers, against Rebel left.

Z, Second position of our artillery, half of the guns against Rebel main battery.

A, Rebels' strong point, defended by main battery and by flank fire from their right.

1, Rebels' weak point, attacked by Col. Smith with 13th Ohio regiment.

for help to arrive. By the time Rosecrans and the others reached the battlefield the entire scene had heated up considerably. A member of the 50th Virginia infantry recalled the effect their artillery had on the Yankees: "...at this time our cannon sent a fearful shot amongst them and did great destruction...boom went the cannon of our enemy, the large balls whistling over our heads, our men flat on the ground, then a volley of musketry would follow and then a round of cannon; then came a terrible shot of shell, it burst and fell all around us...about thirty feet to my right a large chestnut was struck and cut nearly in two...then another, I think a 12 pounder, tore the top of an oak tree to pieces. Just ahead of us, the bullets fell like rain whistling and whizzing over our heads and into the logs we lay behind." [13]

With the battle raging Col. John W. Lowe of the 12th Ohio Infantry, ordered his men to advance to the right and just at that moment an enemy bullet entered the center of his forehead, killing him instantly. As his blood-stained body lay on the ground his legs were shattered with canister shot from the artillery. His body was later found to be mutilated from enemy fire. [14]

The Federal troops made a number of daring, but unsuccessful assaults on the enemy line until nightfall put an end to the fighting at about 7 p.m. Excited by the conflict and believing victory was at hand, General Rosecrans ordered another attack in the mountain darkness. The decision proved to be a poor one. Three Union regiments somehow got themselves in a "U" shape while attempting to maneuver in the night. Suddenly a lone shot rang out which caused the entire group to open fire. When the deed was done it was discovered that the Yankees had killed two and wounded 30 of their own men.

Later that evening General Floyd held a council of war with his officers. He knew the enemy had discovered the weaknesses in his fortifications, and as he was outnumbered nearly three to one he believed that the next day would bring his defeat. Therefore, Floyd ordered a retreat during the night, using Carnifax Ferry and a foot bridge there to cross the Gauley River into Fayette County. Remarkably, this retreat, carried out within short distance of the enemy and over rough terrain, was entirely successful. When the sun rose over the mountain tops on Sept. 11, it found the weary Confederates several miles away. To slow any pursuit the boys in gray destroyed the ferry and footbridge as they left.

Federal troops entered the abandoned Camp Gauley at 6 a.m. They found there Floyd's brigade flag and 25 men of Colonel Tyler's 7th Ohio Infantry who had been captured at Cross Lanes on Aug. 26. They also found several sick and wounded Confederates.

Whitelaw Reid, a young and talented war correspondent for the *Cincinnati Gazette*, accompanied Rosecrans' men on their march and he witnessed the battle of Carnifax Ferry. On the day after the fight Reid filed an excellent report of their arrival at Summersville and subsequent battle: "The clammy fog was still clinging around the faces of the sleepers when the First Brigade was aroused, and by dawn the whole army was on the way. Summersville lay before us eight miles distant. A regiment of rebels was reported...to be holding the town....a rapid march brought us into the single street of Summersville, and the rebels were seen scampering up a hillside beyond...a squad of cavalry dashed out and sent a few shots after them...the General had already ordered forward the column...and had learned from the frightened inhabitants all they knew or were willing to tell of the position, defenses, and strength of the enemy....the column was now near the enemy's lines...Floyd was known to be advised of our approach....Around was spread a lovely variety of hill and dale, pastures and corn fields...all wearing that most smiling of nature's expressions, when ardent summer is just ripening and softening to the mellow richness of autumn. Down the road we knew that a regiment of Ohioans must be coming very near to death; the sun was...flashing on long lines of bayonets...still there came no sounds save the twittering of birds and the rustle of the breeze in the foilage. Suddenly a musket shot, down the road...the skirmishers ...found themselves about two hundred and fifty yards in front of some sort of fortification...For a few moments there was a resumption of sharp but scattered firing, then suddenly there came a terrific clash of musketry and a perfect storm of lead. The enemy had opened along his whole front....our men stood their ground manfully and returned the fire with spirit. The angry peals of musketry, sharp as peals of heavy thunder, grew fiercer, till the sound became one tremendous, incessant roar....at least one full battery of heavy field pieces sent in their swelling, deep-toned notes to mingle with the crashing rattle of small arms...as Colonel Lowe came up...while waving his sword to cheer them on, he was struck in the forehead and fell headlong from his horse....Meantime General Rosecrans...directing the movements ...directed...Hartsuff to bring up the German brigade ....They poured a deadly volley and brought back... accurate information concerning the main rebel redoubt...It was now so dark that it was almost impossible to distinguish the forms of men in the entrenchments...General Rosecrans therefore ordered the troops to fall back...By six o'clock in the morning the old Stars and Stripes were floating over Floyd's headquarters." [15]

Union losses in the engagement were 27 killed, 103 wounded and four missing. The Southerners were more fortunate, having only seven wounded, 17 captured and none killed. By forcing General Floyd to abandon Camp Gauley, General Rosecrans reopened his lines of communication and dealt yet another setback to the Confederate ideal in West Virginia.

Floyd's invigorated but sleepless troops withdrew along the Sunday Road and met with General Wise on the turnpike east of Hawks Nest.

General Floyd was upset that Wise had not sent a greater contingent of reinforcements in time for the battle, even though the Wise Legion was attacked at the same time as Floyd in a brief attempt to flank Camp Gauley. Floyd's anger prompted him to write a letter on Sept. 12, to L.P. Walker, the Confederate Secretary of War.[16] Coincidentally, the Southern authorities at Richmond notified General Lee on that same date that he was authorized to replace Wise: "I am instructed by the President to say that you have authority to transfer General Wise's Legion proper to any other command than that of General Floyd...it being clearly evident that the commands...cannot cooperate...The Wise Legion...will be replaced by orders from here for Colonel Russell's Twentieth Mississippi Volunteers and Colonel Phillips Georgia Legion, both at Lynchburg, to join Floyd." [17]

In the absence of a Yankee pursuit the Confederate armies withdrew an additional 12 miles to a point near the western foot of Big Sewell Mountain. At that time General Floyd determined to hold a war council with Wise: "It becomes necessary that a prompt and definite line of action should be at once determined upon and executed. May I ask the favor of you to come down this evening, and bring such officers as you choose to join us in council. Thus we may determine what is best to be done and put the plan into execution at once." [18]

As a result of their meeting General Floyd issued orders for the entire command to fall back a few more miles to the summit of Big Sewell. That movement was accomplished the next day, Sept. 13. Also issued by General Floyd were orders directing that the Allegheny College, at Blue Sulphur Springs, Greenbrier County, be established as a hospital for their sick and wounded soldiers. [19]

Although circumstances did not permit an immediate pursuit of the Confederates, General Rosecrans did order scouts and spies out into the countryside to determine enemy movements. He also sent two Ohio regiments to the last known camp of the Wise Legion in the mistaken belief that they could prevent a union of the two Southern commands. Those men reached the campsite a full day after their adversaries had departed, finding there only some abandoned equipment and hastily discarded clothing. With Confederate forces regrouping at Big Sewell Mountain and General Rosecrans planning his next move, developments on the Kanawha line remained static for several days. On the Huntersville line however, Generals Lee and Loring were also active during this period, a fact which was unknown to Wise and Floyd until several days later. [20]

CHEATED ON THE MOUNTAIN

On Sept. 1, the rains ceased and sunshine prevailed for three days. Having occupied Cheat Mountain summit since July 16, soldiers of the 14th Indiana Infantry had become bored and were chafing for action. In their wilderness fort they felt isolated from friends, family, and the active campaigns of the war. Indeed, theirs was a rugged outpost duty and not one conducive to good morale or the feeling of having contributed substantially to the war effort. Within one week of their arrival they had been joined on the summit by several regiments including the 24th, 25th, and 32nd Ohio Infantry, and a West Virginia artillery battery. Another factor contributing to their discomfort on the mountain was the fact that most of the local inhabitants sympathized with the Confederacy. Their treachery and hatred kept the soldiers in a constant state of uncertainty. An officer with the 14th Indiana wrote his wife that he kept a pistol and an Enfield rifle with him at all times, even though captains were not supposed to be armed. [1]

Desolate and rugged, with rocks and boulders strewn about, rushing streams, and dense laurel thickets everywhere, Cheat Mountain Fort was a wholly inhospitable and unattractive post. Spread out over the summit, the camp was a sprinkling of white tents and wagons, with felled trees and stumps all around. Pvt. George Lambert of the 14th expressed his dislike for the region in his diary: "The name of this mountain certainly could not have been more appropriate nor more applicable to our situation. For we have been cheated in various ways and at various times since our arrival here....We have to...live on half rations...we are cheated in the weather that is...cold, colder, coldest and rainy, rainier, rainiest. The next cheat is our clothing... some of the boys have to wrap their blankets round them when they appear outside to hide their nakedness." [2]

During some of the heaviest rains of mid-August some of the men built log huts on the mountain. Pvt. John McClure described the dwellings in a letter to his sister: "Our houses are built of spruce fir logs and covered with spruce bark. It is a very good covering and keeps everything dry. We sit by a bright fire in a dry house (shantys we call them) and cook our meals." [3]

Another member of the 14th was surprised how quickly "city-boys" could adapt to rough living: "There were many men...in the Regiment who, until now had never passed a night in the woods, or had never slept from under a good roof, or out of a comfortable bed. To see these men taking their four hours relief from guard duty, laying on the wet ground, rolled up in a blanket...sleeping as soundly as if at home...we were astonished."[4]

Over in the Confederate camp at Valley Mountain, General Lee was also taken with the hardships of mountain warfare. On Sept. 1 he wrote again to his wife: "We have a great deal of sickness among the soldiers, and now those on the sick-list would form an army. The measles are still among them, though I hope it is dying out. But it is a disease which though light in childhood is severe in manhood, and prepares the system for other attacks. The constant cold rains, with no shelter but tents, have aggravated it. All these drawbacks, with impassable roads, have paralysed our efforts..." [5] Two days later with the rains having ceased, Lee was in a more hopeful mood, as we can see from a letter to his son, George Washington Custis Lee: "I feel stronger, we are stronger. The three routes leading east are guarded. The men have more confidence, our people a feeling of security....Rain, rain, rain, there has been nothing but rain....The cold too has been greater than I could have conceived. In my winter clothing and buttoned up in my overcoat, I have still been cold....But there is a change in the weather. The glorious sun has been shining.... The drowned earth is warming. The sick are improving..." [6]

Whenever circumstances allowed soldiers on both sides of the conflict attended church services. On Sept. 1 Pvt. John Chamberlayne of the 21st Virginia Infantry, wrote his family about one such gathering: "This morning the Regt had, a rare chance, a sermon preached to it, and a good one....It was a solemn scene, for seats the hill top, for roof, a still blue sky....In some respects too the scene could remind you of the very book that was expounded; for many emaciated sick, some halting along on sticks, some in the arms of their friends, came and lay along the hill to hear the Word..."[7]

Private Chamberlayne went on to mention that one of his friends, Morris Fontaine, was among the victims of Typhoid Fever. The story of Morris Fontaine is a unique one in that his mother and father traveled from Beaver Dam, Virginia, to Valley Mountain, when they heard their only remaining son was dangerously ill. The Fontaine's other son, Edmund, was killed in July at the battle of First Manassas.

Mary Fontaine kept a record of their perilous journey and subsequent experiences. Though the roads were in terrible condition and they did not know exactly where their son was, the Fontaine's reached Valley Mountain on Sept. 3 having traveled four days. Of course their arrival at camp was a matter of considerable curiosity to the questioning soldiers. Due to the thick, heavy mud on the roads, they abandoned the carriage in which they began their trek and rented a horse. Such a scene as they then presented was rare in the West Virginia wilderness. The two of them clanging and splashing along, Mr. Fontaine on a side-saddle with Mary behind him, her legs tucked up. In this fashion, dirty, worn, and hungry, they reached Lee's camp: "Our approach created great curiosity and amazement, as a woman in this part of the country is a very unusual sight, particularly in camp....I was afraid our arrival would agitate our poor boy, as it did, sadly, so I strove to put on as much calmness and cheerfulness as I could...our dear boy was sadly changed....But I think he will recover now, with God's blessing on our nursing. This is to me the most melancholy place I ever saw....the whole mountain is a mire, and so much sickness that it makes one's heart ache to look on. When we came, in the tent opposite ours were four young men lying side by side sick...there were hundreds of others, on this same mountain, some ill, some dying..." [8]

Mary also said that General Lee and Colonel Washington were very kind to them and that Washington had carried milk to them on several occasions. She wrote that it was by God's grace alone that they stood the trial and that with Lee's help they would soon move their son into a vacant house nearby: "General Lee, who called yesterday, says we can have the house and a carpenter to do some little repairs. Everyone around us is kind and interested for us....The scenery around is wild beyond description and the whole very picturesque — the white tents dotting the mountain sides, it looks like two large villages separated by a ravine..."

Writing from his tent on Valley Mountain on Sept. 2, Richard N. Hewitt of the 42nd Virginia Infantry told his wife that his regiment was greatly reduced in strength by disease. He said they had nine dead, 115 with Typhoid Fever, and 135 with other diseases. This loss amounted to nearly 31 percent of his regiments original strength of 840 men. [9] The situation on the Kanawha line was similar. In late August Lt. Col. John H. Richardson of the 1st Infantry Regiment Wise Legion (later 46th Va. Infantry) reported only 371 men fit for duty from a regiment that just a few weeks prior numbered in excess of 1,000 men. [10]

The West Virginia campaign of 1861 was indeed an inglorious affair. Surprisingly however, Mrs. Fontaine was not as she believed, the only women enduring this dilemma with the soldiers. There were probably at least one-half dozen women among the Confederate soldiers of West Virginia. History records several of these, including Mrs. Betsy Sullivan of Pulaski, Tenn. Known to the troops as "Mother Sullivan," she accompanied her husband's regiment, the 1st Tennessee Infantry, into the war. In 1926 her story appeared on the pages of *Confederate Veteran Magazine*: "Mrs. Sullivan went with the 1st Regiment to West Virginia in General Lee's campaign against General Rosecrans, and thence to Northern Virginia when the regiment was under Stonewall Jackson. She marched on foot with her knapsack on her back through the mountains of West Virginia, slept on the frozen ground, under the cold skies...In a skirmish at Cheat Mountain one member of Company K was killed. Mrs. Sullivan brought the body...in a rude wagon to the nearest railway station, where it was prepared for burial...With sublime self-sacrifice, she shared every hardship..." [11]

Writing in 1885 another veteran recalled that a woman also marched with the 8th Tennessee Infantry: "There was a man whose name was Hare...whose wife, Nancy, accompanied us through all these travels and marches, and remained with her husband in camps in real soldier style. She could walk equal to any soldier....she was treated with great respect... by officers and men alike..." [12]

A sad scene which exemplifies the 1861 West Virginia campaign took place at Huntersville on Sept. 3, as yet another young man lost his life to Typhoid Fever. Here in the lonely, distant military depot of Huntersville, far from family and friends, Pvt. O.D. Neal died at a makeshift Confederate hospital. The captain of his company recorded the event in his diary: "Sept. 3. Tuesday—Very warm. O. D. Neal of my company died about one o'clock this evening. He was an exemplary boy, a good soldier, and died with a lively faith in the crucified Redeemer..." Then this entry the following day: "We paid the last tribute of respect to the remains of our departed friend and fellow soldier O. D. Neal today, burying him on a high hill south from the Huntersville church about 300 paces, with military honors..."[13]

On Sept. 4, the rains began anew and despite that worrisome fact General Lee and some of his subordinates began seriously considering an attack on General Reynolds' army. Lee believed that his men could yet win a great victory if only some paths could be found through the wilderness to attack Cheat Mountain Fort. Hearing that Lee was anxious to find a way of turning the Federal position, John Yeager Jr. a local resident and civilian engineer, set out on his own and discovered the necessary route. After laboring through thickets and crossing ravines for several days, Yeager reached a point south of Cheat summit, where the Yankees had a blockhouse and some earthworks. From that position he felt that Lee's men could successfully attack the enemy. Reporting his findings to Gen. H.R. Jackson at Camp Bartow, Yeager then took Colonel Rust of the 3rd Arkansas Infantry on a second journey to the position. Impressed with what he had seen Colonel Rust immediately informed General Lee of the route. Rust was adamant that the method was now found by which General Reynolds troops could be surrounded and defeated. Further, Rust asked that if Lee made the decision to attack that he be allowed to lead the assault on the summit, a request Lee approved despite the fact that Colonel Rust was another "political officer" with no prior military experience.

Headstone from the forgotten grave of Pvt. O.D. Neal, 16th Tennessee Infantry. A boy of 18 who was one of the hundreds of soldiers that lost their lives in the West Virginia mountains during the war. This stone is now on display at the Pocahontas County Historical Society Museum, Marlinton, W.Va.

At this time Lee's command consisted of about 15,000 men, though many of those were sick. Reynolds had approximately 10,000 soldiers under his command, also with large numbers on the sick-lists. Reynolds was assumed to have about 2,000 men on Cheat Mountain (actually varying from 600 to 3,000) and his total force between that camp and Elkwater was thought to be equal to Lee's. General Lee knew that if an attack were made his columns would be separated by rough terrain with no dependable means of communication between them. Also to be considered was the fact that provisions were so scarce that a long offensive could not be sustained. Any offensive movement must necessarily be of short duration. Still, there was some possibility of surprise at both Cheat Fort and on the western side of the crest. If detailed instructions were given to meet every contingency, and if an attack were carried out on the peak and from both sides of the mountain simultaneously, success was possible.

Lee concluded to fight the battle, his first of the "War For Southern Independence." By Sept. 8, he had developed the plan to the point that he could issue the order. This was done after consultation with, and under the name of, General Loring. Detailed, well-drafted, and simple in form, it was a good order that seemed to address every need. Colonel Rust was secretly to take a column of about 1,500 men to the position he and John

Yeager had selected. At the same time, Gen. S.R. Anderson of Tennessee was to move quietly along a route Lee himself had discovered along the western ridge of Cheat Mountain until reaching the road that led to the summit from the Tygart Valley. Once there he was to occupy that crest and block the road. General Jackson, on the eastern side of the mountain, was to assume a position for a march up the Staunton-Parkersburg Turnpike, after it was cleared of Yankees by Rust. Gen. D.S. Donnelson and Col. Jesse Burks were to be prepared to advance down either side of Tygart River toward Elkwater, with the 21st Virginia Infantry in reserve. Rust was to give the signal for the simultaneous attacks to begin by firing. When he did so, the multi-pronged assault would commence with Jackson advancing up the mountain, Anderson preventing reinforcements from reaching the fort and, if need be, supporting Jackson, and having accomplished that Anderson was to march down Tygart's Valley. Donelson and Burks were to pursue the fleeing enemy; the cavalry covering the extreme left. These movements were expected to take several days and all the men were to wear white strips of cloth as arm badges to prevent them from firing into their own men in the dense forest.

The date set for the advance was Sept. 12. Troop movements were to begin on the 9th. Colonels Gilham and Burks were brought up to the front and several days' rations were issued the troops. The advance order having been issued under Loring's name on the 8th, General Lee addressed the troops in a special order on Sept. 9: "The forward movement announced to the Army of the Northwest...gives the general commanding the opportunity of exhorting the troops to keep steadily in view the great principles for which they contend, and to manifest to the world their determination to maintain them. The eyes of the country are upon you. The safety of your homes and the lives of all you hold dear depend upon your courage and exertions. Let each man resolve to be victorious, and that the right of self-government, liberty and peace shall in him find a defender. The progress of this army must be forward." [14]

Also on the 9th Lee wrote to General Floyd: "Great efforts have been made to place this column in marching condition. Although the roads are continuous tracks of mud...I hope the forces can be united...so as to move forward on Thursday the 12th...I therefore advise you of the probability that on your part you may be prepared to take advantage of it, and if circumstances render it advisable, to act on your side." [15]

Of course Lee had no idea that the battle of Carnifax Ferry was imminent, and circumstances would not "render it advisable" for Floyd to assume the offensive. At Camp Bartow General Jackson issued his own special orders to the men at that post. These orders came under the heading "HEADQUARTERS MONTEREY LINE, NORTHWEST ARMY," and for the assault on Cheat Mountain temporarily reorganized the command structure of his troops. It also stipulated that the men be supplied with "four days' rations of salt meat and hard bread." [16]

At 9 o'clock on the morning of Sept. 10, General Anderson's brigade

began their movements for the attack, as theirs was the longest and most difficult march of the endeavor. With no road to follow the men went single file over ridges, across ravines, and through or up creeks. At 10 p.m. the column halted and scattered for shelter as the cold rain returned. Meantime, General Donelson had started during the afternoon, with orders to march down the right bank of Tygart River, cross several ridges, and eventually descend Becky Run Creek to the Huntersville-Huttonsville road, in rear of the Yankees at Elkwater. Finding the terrain even worse than expected Donelson soon decided to leave his artillery behind. The march was so severe that in some areas his men had to lower themselves down steep declines by holding onto tree branches.[17]

Among the Southern soldiers on this march with Donelson was Pvt. Carroll H. Clark of the 16th Tennessee Infantry. Writing after the war, Clark recalled that the men carried old flint-lock muskets and cartridges of one large lead ball and three smaller balls or buckshot. Their cartridge boxes held 40 rounds and were fastened to their belts alongside percussion cap boxes. After marching for several hours Clark said Col. John Savage, commander of the 16th, heard musket firing out in front, which caused the men to double-time toward the noise. He recalled going a short distance and then passing a cabin on their right, beside which lay two wounded

Yankees. "I was then willing for the war to close" he said, "But late in the evening we marched up on the side of the mountain and remained all night....I thought of home and Mother, but doubted seeing them again. We were in view of the Yank's campfires." [18]

Lee himself went forward on the 11th with Burk's and Gilham's troops, who were under the personal direction of General Loring. Advancing toward Elkwater about eight miles to Conrad's Mill, they skirmished with retreating Federal pickets. This was the first combat that Lee personally saw during the war. Generals Anderson and Donelson made good progress on their separate routes, with Donelson's column capturing about 60 enemy pickets along the way, before retiring for the night on the steep mountainside above Becky Run Creek.

Each of the cooperating columns was at its appointed place before sunrise of the 12th. Lee and Loring, with the brigades of Gilham and Burks plus artillery and cavalry, were near the front and right flank of Camp Elkwater; General Donelson had gained Elkwater's left and rear; Anderson was on the turnpike at the western top of Cheat, had cut the telegraph, and could block reinforcements coming up the mountain from Elkwater, or he could block an attacking column from the fort toward the valley. Colonel Rust had overcome the terrain and had his men on the ridge to the right front of Cheat Fort. Jackson was in position on the eastern side of the mountain.

Early that morning Col. Nathan Kimball, of the 14th Indiana, started three supply wagons from the fort toward Elkwater. Moving less than a mile down the mountain the wagons were intercepted by Rust's men in a brief skirmish. Informed of the ambush, Kimball took two companies toward the scene of action, while also sending a column to open the way to his picket on the path to Elkwater. He did not know that those men had been cut off by Anderson's force. When both Federal columns made contact with the enemy, the Confederates dispersed after some lively skirmishing. In the meantime General Lee and the others waited anxiously to hear a volley from Cheat summit which was to be the signal from Colonel Rust for the combined attacks to begin. The foggy morning passed slowly by and there was no signal from Rust, no sound from Cheat Mountain Fort. Waiting expectantly, Lee heard scattered firing off in the direction of Becky Run and he took off down the ridge toward the valley road. Suddenly there was a clanging of sabres, and the solid thud of horses hoofs pounding the damp earth. Just then a detachment of enemy cavalry dashed by Lee, who was hidden from view just inside the woods. The Yankees were speeding in the direction of the same firing Lee heard, which proved to be some Confederate soldiers who decided to fire their muskets rather than extract the old charge. Almost immediately the Yankees returned, again passing Lee unnoticed. They had met some of Donelson's pickets and were

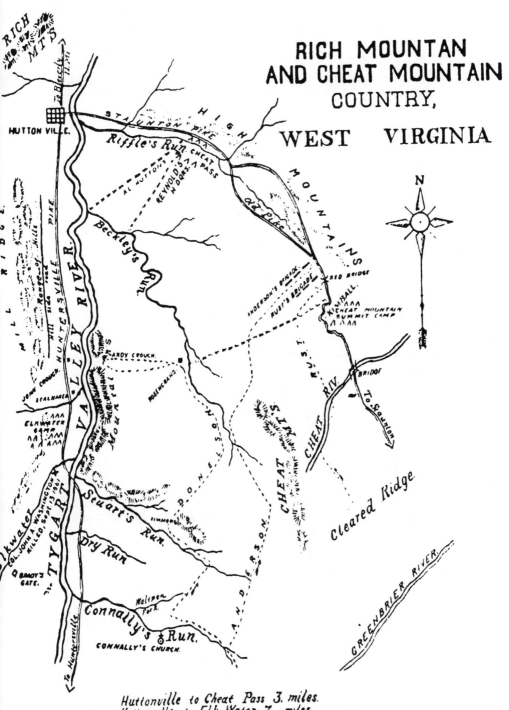

RICH MOUNTAN
AND CHEAT MOUNTAIN
COUNTRY,

WEST   VIRGINIA

Huttonville to Cheat Pass 3. miles.
Huttonville to Elk Water 7. miles.
Cheat Pass to Cheat Mt Summit 9.miles.

Route of Rebel advance...........
Trails or Bridle Paths - - - - -

carrying the news back to their officers. The alarm had been given and the enemy was sure to be on the alert now. Something had obviously gone wrong with Rust's column. Lee realized he must quickly devise a new plan of attack or the entire enterprise was lost. Options were few and Lee determined that all he could do in the absence of support by Rust and Jackson was to make his attack west of the mountain. Accordingly, Lee set about placing his brigades into position for the assault, while also ordering General Donelson to descend into the valley. Anderson was told to withdraw from his exposed position. Lee rode along the column urging officers to get their men in combat order. In the meantime General Donelson captured a few additional pickets. Unfortunately however, Lee soon met resistance from some of his officers. He was told the men were too tired, wet, and hungry to undertake a battle. Further, it was said that Loring could not get into position without crossing the river which was swollen beyond passage. It seemed now that morale was gone. It was noon of the 12th and it was apparent nothing could be accomplished. Lee's first battle was on the verge of collapse. [19]

Pvt. John H. Cammack of the 31st Virginia Infantry explained the mystery of Rust's failure in his postwar memoirs: "I was a volunteer with the 1,600 men who went in the rear of the enemy's camp and fortifications. We were three days and nights getting into position...The place was well fortified, having a blockhouse, with heavy guns in it in the center of the camp and heavy rifle pitts entirely around.... We waded down the Cheat River over five miles, because the laurel was so thick on the banks we could not get through. Sometimes the cold water was up almost to our necks. At nine o'clock the night before the attack, we were a mile and one half from the enemy. Every thread of clothing on us was soaked by the rain and the river....The enemy not knowing we were there sent a large detachment down to relieve picket guard. When they were opposite our company we fired. This alarmed the camp above and they sent probably a thousand men and two pieces of artillery to attack us....At this juncture a council of war was held...3,000 men had come to the enemy the night before. Rust and one other officer favored an immediate attack, but all the others opposed it. Then Colonel Rust began to withdraw his men..."[20]

A participant with the 23rd Virginia Infantry told his wife that they had marched through the mountains "23 miles and had the hardest time you ever saw...wading Cheat River 9 times and wading down the river 2 miles, staid four nights in the woods...went up to attack their camp & found them so strongly fortified that it would be too great..." [21]

To better understand the reasons for the failure of Rust's column, we can refer to the statement of Capt. A.C. Jones of Rust's own 3rd Arkansas Infantry. Jones said the men came suddenly out of the wilderness onto the open road near the fort and there surprised the enemy pickets. The ensuing gunfire, he said, caused Kimball to send reinforcements. He said they may have been able to attack the fort directly had the men been assembled. However, due to the rough nature of the country the men were spread out single file for nearly a mile. "In the meantime," he said, "it became plainly evident that the entire Yankee army was aroused. And so it turned out that all the beautiful plans about surprise and capture...came to naught." [22]

Jones also said that Rust was still reluctant to give up the fight and personally made a reconnaissance so near the fort that he got a bullet through his jacket. Peering as best he could into the camp Rust observed about 3,000 men on full alert scurrying about and going for their weapons. The Confederates had anticipated a much smaller garrison than they found. Jones recalled that a council of officers was held and the decision to withdraw followed. The element of surprise was lost, the enemy was in greater strength than expected, and Rust had no communication possible with his superiors. Jones said there was nothing left to do but return to Camp Bartow.

Rust's men were not alone in skirmishing with the enemy on the mountain. On the eastern approach to the fort Colonel Jackson's men had engaged the Yankees in several brief but hotly contested fights.[23] Why then, did Lee and the others not hear the commotion and believe it to be the attack signal? Again, we can refer to Captain Jones for a plausible explanation: "We were half a mile down the mountain side in a dense forest, which no doubt muffled the sound, and it must have been at least two or three miles on an air line intervening, and the sound did not carry that far..."

After another harsh trek through the mountains Rust's men reached Camp Bartow during the evening of the 13th. At 10 p.m. that night Colonel Rust wrote his official report to General Loring: "...Got there at the appointed time, notwithstanding the rain. Seized a number of their pickets and scouts. Learned from them that the enemy was 4,000 to 5,000 ...strongly fortified...We learned...they were aware of your movements, and had telegraphed for reinforcements...We got near enough to see the enemy in the trenches beyond the abatis....I knew the enemy had four times my force; but for the abatis we would have made the assault....I can only say that all human power could do towards success...failed." Rust also explained that Colonel Jackson's column was still upon the first summit of Cheat Mountain, intending to hold that point until receiving orders from Loring. "My own opinion" Rust said, "is that there is nothing to be gained by occupying that mountain." [24]

General Lee held his positions in the Tygart Valley on the 12th and 13th and during part of the 14th, awaiting some word from Colonel Rust. Finally, during the early afternoon of the 14th, General Loring gave Lee the report sent by Colonel Rust. Subsequent to reading the report Lee

issued a statement to the troops: "Camp on Valley River, Va. Sept. 14, 1861. The forced reconnaissance of the enemy's positions, both at Cheat Mountain pass and on Valley river, having been completed, and the character of the natural approaches and the nature of the artificial defenses exposed, the Army of the Northwest will resume its former position...The commanding general experienced much gratification at the cheerfulness and alacrity displayed by the troops in this arduous operation....that readiness for attack, gives assurance of victory when a fit opportunity offers." [25]

Lee's announcement to the troops did not mention the sad fate of Lt. Col. John Augustine Washington, who was killed while on reconnaissance at Elkwater on the 13th. While awaiting word from Rust, Lee had decided to probe the enemy position at Camp Elkwater in an attempt to discover any weakness in their defenses. Lee's son, Rooney, commanding the cavalry, was ordered to lead the expedition. Rooney, accompanied by Colonel Washington and a cavalry detachment, scouted the country in front of the Union lines. Proceeding cautiously at first, Rooney Lee decided their mission was accomplished and wanted to return. Colonel Washington urged they continue awhile longer, and though it was against his better judgement, Rooney Lee agreed. It was to be a fatal decision.

About one mile in front of Camp Elkwater was a Federal picket post, and about another one-half mile in advance of them was a small Union scouting party, consisting of members of the 17th Regiment Indiana Infantry. These men had advanced beyond the picket to a long narrow defile in which ran Elkwater Fork. The mountain side to the right at this section was covered with dense undergrowth, and was thus enticing as a place from which to ambush the Confederates. Three members of the 17th, Sgt. J.J. Weiler, Cpl. Wm. L. Birney, and Pvt. Wm. L. Johnson, advanced along the road, while at the same time Lee and Washington, with just two other men, moved toward them. Just then Lee and Washington caught sight of an enemy sentinel about a half mile down the valley. "Let us capture that fellow on a gray horse," Washington exclaimed. Directing the two men with them to remain behind, Rooney and Colonel Washington charged down the road. After covering about half the distance the intrepid Southerners found themselves directly opposite Sergeant Weiler and party. Realizing their predicament, Lee and Washington wheeled quickly right across the road, presenting their backs to the Yankees. Without a word spoken the three Indiana soldiers raised their muskets and fired. As it happened all three of the men shot Colonel Washington, who fell from his excited horse as it turned away. Major Lee's horse was wounded and he took off on foot up the bed of the creek. Fortunately for Lee his comrades horse ran toward him. Lee mounted it and made good his escape.

General Lee was greatly pained by the loss of his aide and friend. The next morning, the 14th, Lee sent Col. W.E. Starke to Camp Elkwater under flag of truce to determine Washington's fate. Lee's note of inquiry was addressed to the general commanding U.S. troops at Huttonsville: "Lieutenant Colonel John A. Washington, my Aide-de-Camp, whilst riding yesterday with a small escort was fired upon by your pickets and I fear killed. Should such be the case, I request that you will deliver to me his body, or should he be a prisoner in your hands, that I be informed of his condition..."[26]

Early that morning General Reynolds had ordered the return of Washington's body. Sergeant Weiler, one of the party who killed the colonel, drove the wagon containing his remains. In a short while the exchange was accomplished, and the unfortunate episode passed into history, gone but not forgotten.

Colonel Washington had previously made several successful scouts of the Federal camps near Valley Mountain, apparently using a map from a Northern newspaper which was found on his person. An Ohio soldier who witnessed the taking of Washington's body later described what he saw: "Three balls passed through Washington's body near together coming out from his breast. He fell mortally wounded. Major Lee was unhurt...When reached, Colonel Washington was struggling to rise on his elbow, and, though gasping and dying, he muttered, 'Water,' but when it was brought to his lips from the nearby stream he was dead....Washington's name or initials were on his gauntlet cuffs and upon a napkin in his haversack; these served to identify him. He was richly dressed for a soldier, and for weapons had heavy pistols and a large knife in his belt. He also had a powder-flask, field-glass, gold-plated spurs, gold watch and fob-chain, letters, a map of the country, and some small gold coin on his person. His sword, tied to the pommel of his saddle, was carried off by his horse....Thus early, on his first military campaign, fell John Augustine Washington...the great-grandson of General Washington's brother...and on his mothers side a great-grandson of Richard Henry Lee, Virginia's great Revolutionary patriot statesman. He inherited Mount Vernon, but sold it before the war to an association of patriotic ladies..." [27]

Colonel Washington's pistols were sent by General Reynolds to the Secretary of War, Simon Cameron; the Secretary ordered that Sergeant Weiler be given one of the pistols, and the knife went to Corporal Birney, while Private Johnson received the gauntlets. General Reynolds retained the field glass but eventually gave it to Colonel Washington's son George. Col. Milo Hascall, of the 17th Indiana, took possession of the spurs and powder-flask, and Capt. George L. Rose, of Reynolds' staff, kept a letter through which a bullet had passed. Indeed, many of the Union soldiers rejoiced in having killed such a man as Washington. As if the facts were not grim enough, some men exaggerated the truth in their letters home and to hometown newspapers. A member of the 13th Indiana Infantry wrote his friends back home declaring that they had thoroughly whipped the Rebels. He said they killed not one, but two, prominent Confederates: "...we killed Colonel Washington and General Lee and about 100 men...When the bloody 13th got into them we made them run..."[28] Of course exaggeration was not a trait peculiar to Yankees!

On Sept. 16, General Lee addressed a letter to Miss Louisa Washington, the departed colonels daughter: "...He fell in the cause to which he devoted all his energies, and in which his noble heart was warmly enlisted. My intimate association with him for some months has more fully disclosed to me his great worth...We have shared the same tent, and morning and evening has his earnest devotion to Almighty God elicited my grateful admiration....May God, in His mercy, my dear child, sustain you, your sisters and brothers under this heavy affliction..." [29]

The next day Lee wrote his wife, Mary: "...after waiting three days in front of the enemy hoping he would come out of his trenches, we returned to our position at this place. I can not tell you my regret and mortification at the untoward events that caused the failure of the plan....We met with one heavy loss which grieves me deeply: Colonel Washington accompanied Fitzhugh on a reconnoitering expedition, and I fear they were carried away by their zeal...a volley from a concealed party...Their balls passed through the Colonel's body...I am much grieved..." [30]

Under the same date a letter to the Governor of Virginia: "...I was very sanguine of taking the enemy's works on last Thursday morning....we waited for the attack on Cheat Mountain, which was to be the signal....But the signal did not come. All chance for a surprise was gone. The provisions of the men had been destroyed the preceding day by the storm. They had nothing to eat...and were obliged to be withdrawn. The attack to come off from the east side failed from the difficulties in the way...It is a grievous disappointment I assure you....This Governor, is for your own eye. Please do not speak of it; we must try again. Our greatest loss is the death of my dear friend..."

Douglas Southall Freeman, the premier biographer of Robert E. Lee, insightfully evaluated Lee's first campaign: "Thanks to the extraordinary efforts Lee made with the four small brigades west of the mountains, they were in position to attack on time. So was H.R. Jackson, who had a very short distance to go. Only Rust's change of mind prevented the execution of the plan as Lee had drawn it up. But if the plan had not called for Rust to give the signal, it might have involved some other move equally apt to be upset by unforeseen happenings. In short, the plan of action suggested that Lee was disposed to be overelaborate in his strategy to attempt too much with the tools he had..."[31]

Entered according to act of Congress in the year 1861 by J. Nep Roesler in the Clerks office of the District Court of the Southern District of Ohio

Sketched fr. nature & drawn on stone by J. Nep Roesler Corp'l of Color Guard Comp. G 47th Reg' OV-USA

Printed by Ehrgott, Forbriger & C°, Cincinn.

CAMP, GAULEY BRIDGE.

The Federal camp at Gauley Bridge, W.Va. in 1861. This served as headquarters and supply depot for General Rosecrans' army. Courtesy Fayette County Historical Society

SEWELL MOUNTAIN AND MEADOW BLUFF

*A*bout noon of Sept. 15, General Rosecrans held a council of war at Cross Lanes, near Carnifax Ferry. Gen. Jacob D. Cox later described the meeting: "I rode over from my camp at the Sunday Road...and passing through the field of the recent combat, reached the general's headquarters...I was able to assure him that it was easy for his command to follow the line of march on which Floyd had retreated, if better means of crossing the Gauley were provided....He hesitated to commit himself...McCook's brigade was ordered to report to me as soon as it could be put over the river, and I was authorized to advance some six miles (from Sunday Road) toward the enemy, to Aldersons or Spy Rock...beyond which Sewell Mountain is 14 miles southeast." [1]

General Rosecrans determined to press the advantage won in his battle of Sept. 10, and attempt to push the Confederate forces further south, out of his immediate area of operations. Rosecrans also hoped to occupy the turnpike in the vicinity of Lewisburg, so as to prevent the enemy from regaining that ground. Such a position would also afford him an advanced southern front from which he might attack the railroad further south, or march into the Shenandoah Valley. General Rosecrans' plan of advance was implemented the day after his Cross Lanes conference as General Cox and 5,000 Union soldiers advanced to Spy Rock or present-day Lookout, W.Va., one days' march west of Floyd's camp on Big Sewell Mountain.

General Floyd's scouts brought word on the morning of the 16th that the enemy was advancing. Floyd grew concerned that the Yankees would attempt to flank his position by marching down the Wilderness Road. This old pioneer trail entered Meadow Bluff from the east via Hughes' Ferry on the Gauley River, below Summersville. It would be easy for men in the area of Carnifax Ferry to take that route instead of the James River & Kanawha Turnpike. If the Yankees did so they could conceivably gain the rear of Wise and Floyd. Hoping to prevent that from happening General Floyd ordered the road obstructed: "I think it proper to say to you that it becomes a matter of vital importance to prevent, if possible...the advance of the enemy upon the Wilderness Road...one of the best modes by which it can

Places where Wise's Legion camped.

PLACES WHERE WISES LEGION CAMPED 1861

From Lewisburg to Meadow Bluff 16 mi
" " Frazier's 25 "
" " Top of Big Sewell 30 "
" " Locust Lane 39 "
" " Dogwood Gap 48 "
" " Gauley Bridge 62
" " Charleston Kan. 100
" " Blue Sulp. Spgs. 13
From Charleston to Point Pleasant 57 "
(on the Ohio.)

be done is for you to go down as far as possible on the Wilderness Road with all your force and spare no pains or labor to obstruct it completely....every point should be obstructed where such a thing is possible." These orders were carried out by five companies of the 79th Regiment Virginia Militia, Greenbrier County, commanded by Col. George F. Henry. [2]

Like Rosecrans the previous day, General Floyd determined that a council of war was necessary. At 5 p.m. on the 16th Floyd and Wise, with their attendant staffs, met in council for two hours. General Wise stated that he would like to make an advance down the south bank of the Kanawha River to Charleston. He believed a large force of cavalry and infantry from their combined commands could accomplish the mission and obtain supplies, such as salt, for the army. Wise also made clear his desire to hold their positions on Sewell Mountain for at least a few more days. General Floyd seemed to agree with Wise's plan for the time being and the meeting adjourned. At this point it seems that Floyd either had a change of heart or had intentionally deceived Wise as to his plans. Less than one hour after the meeting he issued orders for their commands to withdraw: "I am instructed by General Floyd to say to you that it has been determined to fall back to the most defensible point between Meadow Bluff and Lewisburg. He will put his column in motion at once. You will hold your command in readiness to bring up the rear." [3]

This apparent deception on the part of Floyd infuriated Wise and he very defiantly refused to budge from his camp, which he appropriately named "Camp Defiance." General Wise was so angered by the move that he wrote Floyd, explaining his astonishment: "...this order to be ready followed immediately after a verbal conference with you, at your request, in which I understood you distinctly as determining to hold, for a time at least, the almost impregnable position which I now occupy...We had hardly ridden to my headquarters...when wagons came moving back...My camp has many sick, some convalescent, and I deem it inhumane to risk the health of these men in this wet weather." [4]

Despite Wise's complaints General Floyd's brigade was marched off into the mountain darkness on a move which certainly could have waited until morning. Some members of the Wise Legion stood in disbelief and watched their comrades disappear into the night. One disgruntled participant in the march told his wife that he had already gone to bed when the order to move was given. He said they left Big Sewell at 11 p.m. and marched 13 hours through rain and mud to Meadow Bluff, a distance of about 14 miles. [5] Adding insult to injury, Floyd's sick troops were left at Sewell Mountain and responsibility for their care fell upon General Wise.

At Spy Rock on the 17th, General Cox was busy trying to supply his command and ordering scouts out toward Sewell Mountain. At this time Cox did not know the exact locations of the Confederates and he pressed

Federal cavalry on Sewell Mountain looking toward General Lee's camp, 1861.
Courtesy Fayette County Historical Society

his cavalry to reach the summit of Big Sewell as soon as possible. Late in the day General Cox sent Rosecrans, who was still at Carnifax Ferry, a dispatch explaining his actions thus far.[6] Cox also wrote to Colonel Tyler, at Gauley Bridge, ordering the establishment of a line of military couriers between Charleston and his headquarters at Spy Rock. He also ordered his commissary department to send additional supplies: "Send us some salt, vinegar, molasses....I shall look for General Rosecrans to be on this line within two days...as soon as Genl. R. comes I shall order you up." [7]

Floyd and Wise were also busy on the 17th entrenching their positions while diligently attempting to resupply and organize their haggard troops. On Sept. 18, General Wise addressed his Legion with a long patriotic speech intended to boost morale. Wise told his men that they must be prepared to fight an enemy superior in numbers by "two or three or several to one," and to expect simultaneous attacks at front and rear. Wise said if anyone in his command was doubtful as to the outcome of such fighting, they could go on to Meadow Bluff, presumably out of harms way. The old governor's speech struck the mark, as a witness described: "The speech, delivered successively to the three regiments of infantry and to the artillery, was received with the wildest enthusiasm. Not one solitary individual in the legion failed to respond, and the spirits of the corps were raised and maintained at the highest fighting pitch." [8]

Frustrated in his attempts to unite forces at Meadow Bluff, General Floyd ordered the militia of Generals Chapman and Beckley, then a days' march west in Raleigh County, to join him "at the earliest practicable moment."[9] The following day, the 19th, General Cox's cavalry reached the western foot of Big Sewell Mountain, about two miles from Wise's position on the eastern crest of Sewell. When scouts reported the enemy advance, Wise grew concerned that his men would soon come under attack. His defensive preparations were yet incomplete and many of his men were absent and in the hospital. Nevertheless, Wise was determined to hold his ground. He wrote Floyd of the developments and told him he planned to "hold on here and fight the enemy, expecting them to attack me." Wise also said he would leave it to Floyd's better judgement whether to send reinforcements or not. [10] Of course given the animosity between these two champions of incompetence, and considering the fiasco at Carnifax, there was no earthly way Floyd was going to send Wise any help. Floyd replied to Wise saying he had known for several days of the enemy advance. He took the opportunity to again ask Wise to join him at Meadow Bluff. Floyd expressed his regret that Wise did not comply with his withdraw order of the 16th. He said that with their forces divided the result could be disastrous and that he hoped Wise would unite with him in a "stand against the enemy at this point." [11]

As you might guess Wise did not agree with his commander's viewpoint. He dictated a boastful letter to Floyd in which he described his ability to whip the Yankees: "I can meet them in the trenches with 1,800 infantry and artillery, and by tomorrow will have my eight companies of cavalry (say 350 to 400) in all, 2,200, with nine pieces of artillery. With this force, posted as I am, I can repulse 4,000."[12]

General Floyd remained unconvinced that Big Sewell was the place to make a stand, and he ordered trenches dug along the eastern bank of Meadow River, about one-half mile west of his headquarters. Pvt. William Clark Reynolds, age 25, and a member of the 22nd Virginia Infantry, described their trenches: "Our regiment worked on the breast works on the right flank of the Meadow River fortifications. Our company had one axe and two butcher knives to work with, so some idea may be formed of the efficiency of our defenses." [13]

Following the failed campaign at Cheat Mountain, General Lee's attention turned to the Kanawha Line and the efforts of Wise and Floyd. Lee determined to go in person to that theater. After conferring with his officers he and his only remaining aide, Colonel Taylor, rode slowly away from the misery and mud of Valley Mountain, never to return. On Sept. 20, General Floyd received a letter from Lee saying that he was then at Frankford, east of Lewisburg: "I have reached this point on my way to your camp. Major Reynolds ...informs me that it is believed the enemy in full force is crossing the Gauley River to attack you...Collect all your force and throw up such breast-works as you can to oppose him...send for General Chapman and Colonel Beckley to cross to your side...all your sick in rear of you ought to be sent well back. I have only a few cavalry with me and shall be obliged to halt for the night this side of Lewisburg." [14]

As had been the case since the beginning of the war, the newspapers, North and South, were generally critical of their military commanders. General Lee was a special favorite of the editors at this time for his perceived complete failure in West Virginia. With Lee's decision to focus on the Kanawha Line, an article appeared in the *Richmond Dispatch* which was typical of the period: "It is clear that the 'forward movement' of General Lee from the direction of Huntersville and Monterey has been blocked...by the enemy. It is plain that some other line of march must be adopted, or else the enemy must be expected to make his winter quarters in Western Virginia....and we must expect one-third of Virginia to remain under the jurisdiction of Pierpont and Carlile, for a season....A mountain frontier is a nursery of assault and invasion....the present campaign in that quarter possesses immense interest to the whole South....The only fear to be apprehended for the success of operations beyond Lewisburg is from the too great circumspection of General Lee....While Lee was weaving ingenious webs of strategy about Cheat Mountain, Rosecrans was legging it down to the Gauley." [15]

General Wise learned that a large detachment of Federal cavalry had occupied the western crest of Sewell Mountain, and on the afternoon of the 20th he decided to advance on their position. For this movement he selected five companies of infantry, or about 250 men. The Union men, commanded by Major Hines, did not realize they had advanced to within one mile of the Confederate camp at the mountain's eastern summit. They mistakenly believed that the nearest enemy force was at Meadow Bluff with Floyd. Advancing but a short distance into the deep ravine that separated the two peaks, Wise and company were suddenly fired upon by the Yankees. Almost instantly a lively skirmish began as the sounds of combat echoed through the mountain defiles and Wise pressed his adversary. Major Hines' men were soon pushed back, steadily losing ground to the intrepid Confederates. Wise became caught-up in the conflict, personally directing the fighting until nightfall put an end to the contest. He had killed one Yankee and pushed the remainder backward two miles. His forces suffered no casualties. That night the Confederates rested as best they could without tents or other shelter.

At dawn the next morning General Wise sent a man back to Camp Defiance to let them know that he was going to press the enemy further. As soon as the fog was off the mountain a rambling skirmish began which continued until noon, when General Wise ordered a return to camp. Arriving at Camp Defiance some four hours later, around 5 p.m., Wise was given a dispatch from General Lee, who had now reached Meadow Bluff. Lee was thoroughly briefed by General Floyd, and he was disturbed to find their forces still divided. Thinking

Gen. Jacob D. Cox, U.S.A.

that he might succeed where Floyd had failed, Lee wrote to Wise in an attempt to unite their commands: "I have just arrived at this camp and regret to find the forces not united...as far as I can judge our united forces are not more than one half of the strength of the enemy....It would be the height of imprudence to submit them separately to his attack...I beg therefore, if not too late, that the troops be united, and that we conquer or die together. You have spoken to me of want of consultation and concert; let that pass until the enemy is driven back, and then, as far as I can, all shall be arranged. I expect this of your magnanimity. Consult that and the interest of our cause, and all will go well." [16]

The obstinate Wise was no more receptive to calls for cooperation from Lee than he had been those of Floyd. In fact, Wise was personally offended by Lee's dispatch, so he fired-off one of his own: "I have just returned from feeling the enemy, being out all night...but, wet, weary, and fatigued as I am, your note reads so much like a rebuke... that I do not lose a moment without replying....In the first place, I consider my force united with that of General Floyd as much as it ever has been...Floyd has about 3,800, and I about 2,200 men, of all arms, and of these at least 5,500 are efficient....The two roads and the two positions had perhaps better be examined, I respectfully submit, before my judgement is condemned."[17]

Receiving Wise's dispatch late that evening, Lee decided to accept his ornery subordinates advice and inspect Camp Defiance personally. The next morning, the 22nd, Lee and Colonel Taylor rode forward to Big Sewell Mountain, where another skirmish was then in progress. General Wise and staff met Lee and Taylor near the headquarters tent, greeting them cordially. Impressed with the sight of General Lee, a witness to the meeting later recalled the event: "I had never seen him, and knowing our critical position I was anxious for his presence. The day of his arrival I was on the skirmish line and it was unusually hot....I returned to camp and saw him...there was a kindliness in his expression most unusual in one possessing eyes so dark and brilliant. He was dignified and courtly...he appeared so unconscious of his merits, so courteous, so kind, that anyone who approached him must have felt that Lee was his...friend."[(18)]

Lee and Wise spent several hours inspecting the camps and fortifications at Sewell Mountain. Although Lee did find the position to be a naturally strong one, as Wise had said, there were a number of side roads or trails by which an attack could be launched against it. Late in the afternoon Lee left Camp Defiance. He did not order Wise to retreat, and Wise took this as a vindication of his judgement. In point of fact, Lee still preferred to meet the Yankees at Meadow Bluff. It was early in the conflict and Lee was not yet a firm commander. Had these events transpired late in 1862 or 1863, Lee would undoubtedly have been more forceful in handling his subordinates. [(19)]

After the fighting of the 21st, General Cox ordered his cavalry back to Spy Rock, and he notified General Rosecrans of the movements and locations of the enemy. Cox also said he wanted to advance his entire force of 5,000 men to the Sewell Mountain range. Rosecrans approved the advance, telling Cox to be careful not to fall into a "Rebel trap." Cox then issued orders for the march to Sewell to begin at 9 a.m. of Sept. 23.[(20)]

When the Federal vanguard ascended the western crest of Big Sewell Mountain it caught the Confederates off guard. Wise told one of his cavalry officers, Col. Nat Tyler, to notify General Lee of the enemy advance: "I am directed by General Wise to say that the enemy in very heavy columns has occupied the top of Sewell Mountain. Infantry, cavalry, and artillery are all plainly visible from our camp, about one mile distant..." [(21)]

General Floyd told Lee that he believed the movement on Sewell to be a diversionary tactic, while the main body of the enemy attacked him at Meadow Bluff. Such an attack was possible along the Wilderness Road. Fortunately, however, Floyd had earlier ordered the obstruction of that route making enemy movements there extremely difficult.

General Lee responded immediately to Wise's notice, telling Wise to send all of his wagons to the rear and to decide whether or not his forces were sufficient to withstand an assault. Lee explained the concern about possible enemy movements via the Wilderness Road, and he told Wise that he had cavalry out checking the road at that time. (22)

It was well into the night when Wise received Lee's correspondence and he replied at midnight. He said he could not retire his baggage wagons or other incumbrances, adding that the enemy were at least 3,000 strong. Wise also dismissed the notion of a Yankee advance along the Wilderness Road, saying the idea was "simply absurd," and adding that he felt "compelled to stand here and fight as long as I can endure and ammunition lasts. All is at stake with my command, and it shall be sold dearly."(23)

Spending a restless night at Meadow Bluff, Lee replied to Wise at 4 a.m. of the 24th: "...send word whether you have sufficient ammunition, and any information as to the operations of the enemy that may serve to regulate the movements of General Floyd." Lee also expressed his anxiety to General Wise as to the precarious situation he faced. Lee said he regretted the fact that Wise felt compelled to make a stand because "at the distance you are from support it may jeopardize the whole command."(24)

Wise replied at 7:15 a.m., telling Lee that his camp had been busy all night and stating emphatically that the enemy was moving strictly on Camp Defiance and not on Floyd at Meadow Bluff. He said three of his soldiers had been wounded and that the previous days' fighting had continued until nightfall. Then, like a criminal who finds salvation "in the shadow of the noose," Wise indicated he would cooperate if Lee ordered him to retreat. He said that if so ordered his wagons should be emptied of baggage and used to haul ammunition and supplies.(25)

Of course Lee knew that it would be risking disaster to order a retreat in the face of the enemy. Hoping to gain reinforcements from the Army of the Northwest, Lee sent a message to General Loring who was then encamped at Marlings Bottom or present-day Marlinton, not far from Huntersville. Lee explained the situation and requested that Loring send help "without delay."(26)

Fearing that a decisive battle was at hand, and not wanting to leave its conduct to a politician, Lee determined to once again take the road to Sewell Mountain. Taking with him four of Floyd's infantry regiments and two pieces of artillery, Lee and Taylor began their 14 mile journey. A courier was sent ahead to inform Wise that help was coming and to encourage Wise to send all of his baggage wagons away from the field of action. Still doubtful that the true intentions of the enemy had been determined, Lee said he was advancing to Wise's support "In ignorance of the movements of the enemy on our flanks."(27) In actuality General Wise had been correct. The Yankees made no attempt to advance in force along the Wilderness Road.

With help for Wise on the way, General Cox ordered the flanks of

Camp Defiance examined in the hope of discovering some weakness in the enemy line. Cox ordered his artillery and several companies of infantry to occupy the Confederates in front, while his scouts probed their defenses. At 9 a.m. Cox's infantry plunged excitedly into the great ravine that separated the opposing armies, while the Federal artillery poured forth an impressive but ineffectual barrage of iron and lead. General Wise counter-attacked in front, not suspecting his adversaries true motives. For several hours the smoke and confusion of battle prevailed as the entire scene became more of a general engagement than a skirmish. One of the Southern combatants later wrote that the fighting was conducted from tree to tree and that his regiment was poorly armed at the time. He said they had flint-lock muskets and "bowie-knives about 20 inches long." [28]

The contest continued into the afternoon and at 2 p.m. Lee and the long column of reinforcements arrived on the mountain. Shortly thereafter the clash was brought to a close. Confederate losses included one dead and several wounded. Cox's men suffered several wounded and no reported deaths. It seems odd that a fight which "sounded" fierce should result in so

GEN. ROBERT E. LEE
Near here, at highest point on the Midland Trail, Gen. Robert E. Lee had headquarters during his campaign in West Virginia in 1861. His famous war horse, "Traveler," was brought to him here from the Andrew Johnston farm in Greenbrier County.

little harm to either army. Witnesses recalled that the artillery on both sides almost always overshot their targets, and apparently the "Indian-style" fighting did not lend itself to accuracy.

General Lee found himself at Sewell Mountain not by his own choosing, but due to Wise's unyielding character and the advance of the enemy. There must have been for Lee a sense of foreboding, having replaced one gloomy mountain camp with another. There was absolutely nothing at Camp Defiance to relieve any such feeling. All Lee could do was to throw himself into the task at hand and pray for victory.

During the evening of the 24th, General Floyd received some reinforcements of his own, with the arrival at Meadow Bluff of the 20th Regiment Mississippi Infantry, commanded by Col. Dan R. Russell. This elevated the Southern force at that camp to about 1,900 men. That evening General Lee bivouacked on the mountainside covered only by his overcoat, because the wagon containing his personal effects did not arrive until Sept. 26. It was thus at this time that Lee began to grow the beard that would become so familiar to Americans as the classic image of Robert E. Lee.

Lee arose early on the morning of the 25th and he wasted no time in examining the Union encampment with his binoculars. He and Colonel Taylor were seen walking slowly along the ridge facing the enemy, after which Lee notified General Floyd of his findings: "Everything is quiet in the enemy's camp. I can count five or six regiments, but cannot see ground in their rear where others may be....I suppose if we fall back the enemy will follow. This is a strong point, if they will fight us here." It seems that Lee had now reconciled himself to making a stand at Camp Defiance. He asked Floyd, "How would it do to make a stand here?" and added "In that event we shall require provisions and forage. Of the latter there is none, and the horses are suffering... send three days rations of flour, salt, and bacon, if you have it...send also sugar and coffee..."[29]

At about noon of the 25th, General Cox ordered the 11th Ohio Infantry out on reconnaissance to the right of Camp Defiance. Moving through the tangled undergrowth of the dense forest, the Ohioans had not gone far when Confederate pickets opened fire. Hearing the commotion General Wise was quick to respond, personally leading a strong force of skirmishers out to check the enemy advance. Desultory firing continued for several hours when, at about 4:30 p.m., a courier gave General Wise a dispatch from Confederate President Jefferson Davis: "Sir...You are instructed to turn over all the troops heretofore under your command, to General John B. Floyd, and to report yourself in person to the Adjutant General in the city of Richmond, with the least delay. In making the transfer to General Floyd, you will include everything under your command."[30]

Though the order was explicit, Wise debated whether to defy President Davis, just as he had already defied Floyd and Lee. After conferring with General Lee, Wise decided to comply with the President's order, announcing his recall to the troops. The feisty old governor packed his baggage immediately and departed for Richmond the next morning. He was accompanied on his ride by his son, Capt. Obadiah Wise, and four members of his staff. [31]

As the despondent General Wise rode away from Sewell Mountain on the 26th, General Rosecrans finally arrived at the camp of General Cox. He discovered upon arrival that there existed insufficient supplies of food for the men and forage for the animals. Additionally, there were large numbers of sick troops both in camp and in homes and barns along the road, all the way back to Gauley Bridge, 32 miles in the rear.

Selecting a company of infantry to assist them, General Rosecrans and his officers personally surveyed Lee's camp. This mission was conducted in cold rain and strong winds which would prove to be a deluge of three days duration. The inundation was unprecedented and disastrous. Disease and supply problems, which were already at near intolerable levels in both camps, became many times worse before the rains ended. The oppressive storms prompted General Floyd to tell Lee that "at this season of the year, I do not remember to have seen such a storm in the mountains of Virginia. It has put an almost absolute stop to all locomotion." Indeed the rains had further damaged the areas roads. One witness said that where part of the road had been there were now "gullies eight or ten or even fifteen feet deep."[32] Testifying on the conduct of the war in 1865, General Rosecrans stated that during this storm 18 horses died in one night at his headquarters. [33]

Lee had requested additional reinforcements from Floyd and he sent up to Camp Defiance the 20th Mississippi Infantry. They reached the camp at 10:00 p.m. of the 26th, during the worst of the storm, the rain having turned into sleet. A veteran of the 20th Mississippi later claimed that it took three days for their tents and other supplies to arrive on the mountain. He said they slept, or tried to sleep, that entire time without shelter. As a direct result of these numerous and unfortunate hardships his regiment suffered a loss by disease rate in excess of 60 percent during the Sewell Mountain campaign. [34]

General Floyd's command at Meadow Bluff now consisted of the 36th, 50th, and 51st Virginia Infantry Regiments; about 1,000 men. Lee's force was about 5,000 strong with an additional 3,000 soldiers under General Loring on their way. When General Rosecrans had come up he brought another 3,000 men to General Cox, boosting his army to 8,000, with about 5,200 effective.

That night Lee wrote a letter to his wife, Mary: "...I have but little time for writing tonight, and will, therefore, write to you...I infer you received my letter written before leaving Valley Mountain....It is raining heavily. The men are all exposed on the mountain, with the enemy opposite us.... for two nights I have lain buttoned up in my overcoat. Today my tent came up and I am in it. Yet I fear I shall not sleep for thinking of the poor men..."[35]

The three-day storm also effected troops on the Huntersville line. An

Indiana soldier at Camp Elkwater said exposure to the rain and sleet caused the death of fifteen horses and two men in one night at that camp.[36] The downpour caught the reinforcements under Loring on the march, further complicating an already arduous expedition. When Loring gave the order to reinforce Lee, he left camp in such a rush that his supply wagons

A 1928 view of the "Lee Tree" under which General Lee's tent was pitched during the Sewell Mountain campaign, Sept./Oct. 1861. In 1936 this tree was struck by lightning and subsequently cut down. Another was planted on the exact spot by the United Daughters of the Confederacy.
Courtesy Floyd McClung, Hugheston, W.Va.

Lee and Traveller at Petersburg, Va., 1864. Courtesy Washington & Lee University

were not yet assembled. A soldier from Tennessee related the event: "...we left in haste without transportation for tents or trunks or anything else save cooking utensils en route for Lewisburg..." [37]

Loring's column reached Lewisburg on Sept. 27, and passed through that town four miles, to Bungers Mill. Many of Loring's men were impressed with the beauty of Lewisburg and surrounding country. Tom Penn, of the 42nd Virginia Infantry, told his sister that Lewisburg "burst upon our view just after climbing a long and rough mountain, from the top of which we had a splendid view of the large nice farms and beautiful residences...below...The scenery created a momentary change in the feeling of every soldier who ascended the mountain almost worn out with fatigue...and the air was made to ring for miles around with shouts...we unfurled the banner and proudly marched through the neat village...keeping up a continuous shout, and greeted everywhere by nice young ladies who waved their handkerchiefs from nearly every window..."[38]

The normally quiet and attractive city of Lewisburg was the scene of frequent military activity, as described by Pvt. G.A. Cox of the 8th Virginia Cavalry: "...we went to Lewisburg...but provisions were scarce there and not only that, but there is so much confusion and a great many sick soldiers there, and the streets are always crowded with soldiers passing to and from the army..."[39]

On the afternoon of the 27th, General Floyd notified Lee of Loring's arrival in Greenbrier County, and said too that he had forwarded to Camp Defiance all the supplies which wagons could be found to carry. Floyd was not in favor of Lee's inclination toward making a stand at Sewell Mountain. He said the condition of the roads and the increased distance to Sewell from Lewisburg, their supply base, would make it increasingly difficult to hold that position. Floyd remained firmly convinced that Meadow Bluff was the most defensible point between Sewell and Lewisburg. Unlike Wise however, he did express his desire to cooperate, telling Lee that he would leave the decision to his better judgement.

As the rains poured, and the Confederates consolidated, the Yankees at Sewell fared little better than their counterparts. Maj. Rutherford B. Hayes of the 23rd Ohio Volunteer Infantry, wrote his wife saying they were "...in the midst of a very cold rain storm...rain for fifteen hours; getting colder and colder, and still raining. In leaky tents, with wornout blankets, insufficient socks and shoes, many without overcoats. This is no joke." [40]

Early the next morning, the 28th, the precipitation was still very much in evidence, and Floyd wrote Lee advising him that high water had damaged or destroyed two bridges between their camps. This of course blocked the forwarding of supplies.[41] The bad weather also kept General Lee near his tent, where he spent many hours conferring with his officers and receiving an occasional guest. Lee's aide, Colonel Taylor, later wrote a description of the headquarters on Big Sewell Mountain: "One solitary tent constituted his headquarters camp; this served for the general and his aide; and when visitors were entertained, as actually occurred, the general shared his blankets with his aide, turning over those of the latter to his guest. His dinner service was of tin, tin plates, tin cups, tin bowls, everything of tin, and consequently indestructible; and to the annoyance and disgust of the subordinates, who sighed for porcelain, could not or would not be lost."[42]

At 5 p.m. of the 28th, Phillips Legion of Georgia Cavalry and Riflemen arrived at Meadow Bluff, on their way to join Lee. This Georgia Legion was approximately 400 strong. Just two hours later General Loring's column reached Floyd's camp, bringing two regiments and a battery of artillery. Trailing Loring's group by about 12 hours was Gen. S.R. Anderson, and the remainder of the reinforcements, consisting of the 1st, 7th, and 16th Regiments Tennessee Infantry. Loring had brought the 42nd and 48th Regiments Virginia Infantry. Like Loring, Gen. Samuel Read Anderson was a veteran of the Mexican War. He was 57 years old, and prior to the war, served as postmaster at Nashville, Tenn.

On Sunday the 29th the rains stopped and the warm sun rose over the mountains like a gift from God. The weary, wet soldiers sprang to life rejoicing in a sunny day. Over in the Federal camp Rutherford Hayes penned a letter to his wife: "A beautiful bright Sunday morning after a cold, bitter, dismal storm of three days...We are compelled now by roads and climate to stop and return to the region of navigable waters or railroads. No teams can supply us here much longer. In this state of things we shall probably be content with holding the strong points already taken without fighting for more until another campaign." [43]

Major Hayes' impression that the campaign at Sewell was nearing an end was accurate. The season was advanced, the weather getting worse, the sick lists growing, and ample supplies were unheard of for Blue and Gray alike. Of course these facts were not lost on Lee or Rosecrans, and both men hoped the enemy would attack them in their entrenched camps. In the rough mountain terrain it was better to receive an attack than to deliver one, and both commanders continued to prepare for that contingency.

During the 29th reinforcements reached General Rosecrans, in the form of the 13th, 23rd, and 30th Regiments Ohio Infantry. These men were led by Gen. Hugh B. Ewing and Col. E.P. Scammon. At Camp Defiance General Loring and his force of 3,000 men arrived from Meadow Bluff, as did an additional artillery battery under Capt. John H. Guy. General Lee was pleased to receive the additional manpower, but their presence at his camp caused more supply problems. He wrote to Floyd saying that he would now require 50 barrels of flour per day, plus food for the horses.

Lee was now growing concerned that General Rosecrans would not attack. If he did not, Lee must, and he told Floyd that with enough supplies they "might drive the enemy over the Gauley."[44] And again the next day, the 30th, Lee wrote General Floyd, saying that "I begin to fear the enemy will not attack us. We shall therefore have to attack him."[45]

Oct. 1 dawned clear and pleasant, the third consecutive day of good weather. General Rosecrans' commanders now began to express open opposition to remaining in their present predicament. The officers said it was time they returned to their supply base at Gauley Bridge. Rosecrans was against a withdrawal, saying they should remain patient and await General Lee's attack. As these events transpired an article appeared in the *Cincinnati Daily Enquirer* criticizing General Rosecrans' conduct of the campaign: "The inspiring vision of advance through Western Virginia on Staunton, and down to Richmond; or of advance to Cumberland Gap, seizure of the Tennessee and Lynchburg Railroad...all fade away before the dull reality that the roads are becoming impassable, and that General Rosecrans and his subordinates, instead of meditating bold movements to warmer climates, are already talking of hunting up winter quarters in the neighborhood of Charleston." [46]

General Floyd arrived in person at Camp Defiance on Oct. 1. He left a small detachment of cavalry at Meadow Bluff, with Col. James L. Davis in charge. The army under Lee's command was now approximately 9,000 men and as many as 20 cannons. On Oct. 2, the cold rain returned, much to the chagrin of everyone. Just when the poor soldiers thought conditions could not get any worse, they did. A member of the 14th Regiment North Carolina Infantry would later recall that "A great epidemic of sickness broke out among us and nearly everyone was taken sick...the regiment of over one thousand men, only stacked 56 guns at one time...many died in their tents and were buried on the roadside." [47]

With the deadly rain pouring and sharp gusts of wind whipping across the top of Sewell Mountain, Capt. John Buford of the 42nd Virginia Infantry, sat in his tent and read a somber letter from his father: "I suspect you were all rather glad to change quarters...from that at Valley Mountain.... I shouldn't think Big Sewell or Little Sewell would furnish very comfortable quarters. Yet, I hope and trust, the change will be beneficial...I never read of the sickness and hardships of you all that my eyes don't fill and flow with tears. I do not think our revolutionary fathers could have suffered more in every way than our soldiers in the North West."[48]

The situation remained static during Oct. 3rd although there did seem to be increased activity in the Federal camp. Using his binoculars Lee watched the enemy movements and believed an attack was imminent. He ordered all of his wagons loaded and sent to the rear, and at 8 p.m. of the 3rd, Lee issued orders to prepare for action: "The commanding officers of brigades & corps will cause their several commands to be inspected this evening & will see that their arms and ammunition of the men are in perfect order for service. They will also see that all their effective force are at their posts." No attack came on the 4th and the anxious Confederates spent another long, slow day on the alert.[49]

Sunshine and calm weather greeted the troops on Oct. 5. This day was handled the same as the previous two; in hourly expectation of a fight. Unfortunately, or perhaps fortunately, for the vigilant General Lee, there would be no battle. After several days of badgering by his officers, General Rosecrans ordered a retreat. The road in his rear was kept busy all day on the 5th as his sick troops and spare baggage wagons were moved back to Spy Rock. Late that evening nearly 6,000 Union soldiers began their retrograde movement under cover of darkness. The disappointed Yankees were led away from the summit a section at a time. General Cox recalled the scene in his postwar memoirs: "Tents were struck at ten o'clock in the evening, and the trains were sent on their way under escort at eleven...my own brigade was assigned rear guard. We remained upon the crest of the hill until half past one, the men being formed in line of battle and told to lie down until time for them to march... When at last day broke, we were only three or four miles from our camp of the evening before..."[50]

Concerned that their retreat would be discovered, the rear guard troops with General Cox wasted no time in getting off the mountain. They were obliged to wait several hours until the others had started, and they became so anxious to leave that when their turn finally came their movement resembled more of a rout, than an orderly retreat of unbeaten troops. Writing in 1873, Gen. Henry Benham said the men destroyed large quantities of supplies and overturned wagons to speed their flight.[51]

Lee's heart must have sank when he awoke on Oct. 6 to find his opponents gone. Confederate pickets had heard and reported noise from Rosecrans' camp during the night, but it was dismissed by the officer of the guard as nothing unusual. A small detachment of cavalry was quickly sent in pursuit but returned after going only two or three miles. Their horses were weakened by the lack of forage, and in some areas their retreating foe had blocked the road with trees and brush.

The mood of the men at Camp Defiance was one of disbelief and anger. They had hoped this "unnatural war" would soon be over, and they realized there could be no conclusion without fighting. Another factor contributing to their despair was the rapid approach of winter. There was no comfort in the thought of having to remain much longer in this desolate, bleak camp. Writing on Oct. 7, a member of the 42nd Virginia Infantry told his mother of their unhappy predicament: "There seems to be dread...of being caught in these mountains by winter. Our enemies were not as numerous as we supposed them to be...I believe we could have entirely defeated them. Too much caution has lost us the opportunity of a signal victory....It was stated by those sent out on observation that the enemy was strongly fortified, when the truth was they did not throw up fortifications at all."[52]

General Lee quickly drafted a new plan of advance. Lee now wanted General Floyd to advance to the south side of the Kanawha River in an attempt to cut the communications of the enemy on the Gauley. The proposition was that once Floyd had his men in place, Lee would come up with Loring's troops to help drive the Yankees out of the Kanawha Valley.

With General Lee working on the new plan and conferring with his officers, he was once again criticized by the newspapers. Typical of the articles at this time was one which appeared in the *Richmond Examiner*: "One favorable opportunity to expel the enemy has been lost. Shall we lose another? General Lee is able and accomplished....After two disasters to our arms in that section, he may well have been cautious lest a third should finally ruin our interests there. But excess of caution...has wrought, by mere delay, much of the mischief that was dreaded from defeat. The general, we doubt not, now feels the necessity of a more adventurous policy..." [53]

A South Carolina newspaper, the *Charleston Mercury* was even more critical of Lee: "Poor Lee! Rosecrans has fooled him again. Are the roads any worse for Lee than Rosecrans? The people are getting mighty sick of this dilly-dally, dirt digging, scientific warfare; so much so that they will demand that the Great Entrencher be brought back and permitted to pay court to the ladies." [54]

Of course General Lee knew more of the reality of the situation than did the editors of newspapers. On Oct. 7, Lee wrote to Mrs. Lee telling her of the enemies escape. Commenting on the bad press he received, Lee said, "I am sorry, as you say, that the movements of the armies cannot keep pace with the expectations of the editors of the papers. I know they can regulate matters satisfactorily to themselves on paper. I wish they could do so in the field... I hope something will be done to please them..."[55]

BATTLE OF BARTOW

*L*earning that the Confederate forces of Gen. H.R. Jackson were entrenching their camp on the Greenbrier River, about 12 miles from Cheat Mountain, Union Gen. J.J. Reynolds ordered an attack. The date selected for the engagement was Oct. 3rd. Reynolds' troops at Elkwater were called up and combined with those already at Cheat Fort to form an attacking force 5,000 strong. These included the 7th, 9th, 13th, 14th, 15th, and 17th Regiments Indiana Infantry; the 24th, 25th, and 32nd Ohio Infantry; three companies of cavalry from Indiana, Michigan, and Ohio, and 16 artillery pieces formed from three separate artillery units.

Hoping to attack Camp Bartow at sunrise of Oct. 3rd, the Federal troops were assembled at Cheat Fort and placed on the march before midnight of the 2nd. The night was clear and cool, the men anxious for a fight. With bayonets shining in the moonlight the excited boys in blue made their way calmly and methodically down the zig-zag road descending Cheat Mountain to the valley below. Now and then a frightened deer could be heard leaping away through the underbrush, and the haunting screams of wildcats combined with the low calls of great horned owls, rendering the entire scene surrealistic.

Reaching the valley road at 5 a.m., members of the 32nd Ohio Infantry heard voices to their front and through the mountain darkness could discern several shadowy images nearing them. Quickly taking refuge behind a large log, the men in the lead waited nervously for a better look at the ghostly figures. A member of the 32nd related the event: "We saw dimly...an armed man walking—then another—then a third. I now was confronted by my first military problem. What should I do?....If they were scouts they must be captured with as little noise as possible, and I decided to try this myself. Slipping quietly over the log, I started cautiously to intercept them. Bravely enough I prepared to cover them with my pistol, but to my surprise a strange rebellion took possession of my legs. They wobbled like two sticks trying to support a load. This feeling increased the farther I got from our log. I had the men covered with my pistol...They grew in my eyes to at least seven feet in height. I tried to order them to halt, but my mouth would not go off...then my mouth let loose....I demanded to what regiment they belonged. The tall sergeant replied 'the 13th Indiana. What is yours?'"[1]

Arriving within one mile of Camp Bartow at 7 a.m. of the 3rd, Reynolds' men were attacked by an advance guard of the Confederates, 100 strong and concealed in the trees to the right of the turnpike. These men were commanded by Col. Edward Johnson of the 12th Georgia Infantry, and Lt. W. Gibson of the 3rd Arkansas Infantry. When the firing began the Federal column deployed into line of battle and moved straight in. Though vastly outnumbered, the bold Southerners held their ground and kept the lead flying. Colonel Johnson was directing the action near the woodline when all of a sudden his white horse tumbled to the earth, victim of a Yankee bullet. A hot contest was kept up for nearly an hour when six artillery pieces were brought to bear on the Confederates. This act had the desired effect, as Johnson's men were slowly driven back, fighting bravely all the way. Flanked on the right by a battalion of infantry, part of Johnson's force was cut-off and 13 captured. One member of the advance guard was killed and several wounded as they moved slowly back on their entrenchments in good order.

The Confederate camp at Bartow was situated in the foothills of the Allegheny Mountains, just above the south fork of the Greenbrier River, astride the Monterey Turnpike. At the time of the battle the defensive works were incomplete, but those that were ready had been dug into a series of low ridges facing the river. From that vantage point an excellent field of fire could be had for some distance up the Cheat Mountain road, and a branch road northward. The infantry field works were a series of rifle pits along the ridge tops, with a deep trench dug alongside the river below. The camps were established in the rear of the works, and extended to either side of the Monterey Pike.

Advancing to within 700 yards of Camp Bartow, the Northern artillery promptly took position and opened fire. Reynolds' men used eight artillery pieces for the fight, General Jackson's used five. The earth shook and the valley echoed with the sounds of battle. Both sides cut loose a terrific barrage of shot and shell that ripped up the trees and plowed the earth. Col. John Wilder of the 17th Indiana Infantry, said he moved his regiment into "line of battle across an open field, while the battery took position in our rear." And when the battery was ready to fire he moved his men to the right, and "then such a roar of cannon! The first gun fired by the enemy threw a twelve pound ball directly over my head; the wind of it taking my cap off. The ball struck the earth within ten feet of General Reynolds who was in the rear." [2]

General Reynolds ordered his regiments to spread out across the wide valley and push forward in an attempt to flank the enemy. General Jackson

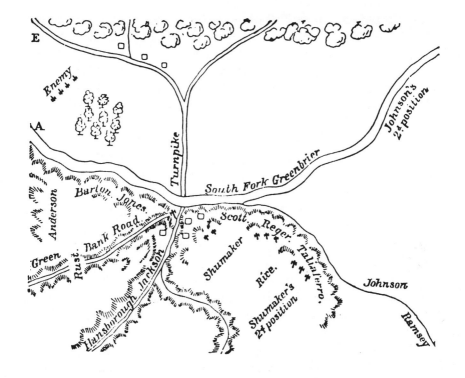

General Jackson's official map of the battleground at Bartow, W.Va.
The letter "A" marks the spot of a Union Army flank attempt, and letter "E"
indicates the road to Cheat Mountain. From the Official Records, *vol. 5*

anticipated the move and deployed some men to both flanks. His extreme right was held by the 1st and 12th Georgia Infantry Regiment's. His center was held by the 23rd and 44th Virginia Infantry, assisted by the 25th Battalion Virginia Infantry. On the left was the 3rd Arkansas, 31st Virginia, and Hansbrough's Battalion, Virginia Infantry. Including artillery Jackson had fewer than 2,000 men against Reynolds' 5,000. The 52nd Virginia Infantry was encamped south of Bartow several miles, at the top of Allegheny Mountain. They took no part in the fighting, arriving too late to help.[3]

Pvt. John Henry Cammack, a 17-year-old member of the 31st Virginia Infantry, described the fighting on the Confederate left flank: "Two of our cannons fired over our heads about fifteen feet above us on the side of the mountain. The gun just above me fired 85 times...My hearing was badly injured by the noise. A gunner in the company next to me performed a very heroic action during the fight. The enemy was throwing shells at us. One fell above the rifle pits and rolled down among the men...This gunner grabbed the shell and threw it out just 2 seconds before it burst."[4]

Several times during the battle, the Northern troops attempted by various methods to flank Jackson's command. Each time the effort was thwarted by the skillful and timely counter actions of the Confederates. Seeing that little could be accomplished by infantry, General Reynolds waited and watched as the fighting evolved into an artillery duel. The Federal artillery was apparently well served, forcing their opponents to change position after every third shot. A Union participant said the "fight came on so gradual that we didn't get much excited. There was more excitement during our musketry skirmish than any other time. After the cannonading commenced, we had as much fun, laughing, talking and joking, as if we had been in camp."[5]

Hoping to take a more active role in the fighting, some Northern infantry officers asked General Reynolds for permission to storm the center of the Southern line. Reynolds refused, saying it would be too great a sacrifice of life. He had gained nothing through several casualty-laden flank attempts, and he realized that an attack on the center, Jackson's strongest point, was also likely to fail.[6]

Reynolds' flank attempts were described by a young soldier from Georgia: "...they tried to flank us on our left Col. Rust with his Arkansas boys met them and they tried the right flank...the 12th Georgia...was ordered across the river to meet them we went in a run, waded the river near waist deep...were then ordered back again...and ordered to get in this ditch...not to fire until we could see the whites of their eyes...the balls went Zip all around us... one of the cannon opened on them with grape shot and they retreated in quick time...thus ended the first battle I was ever in." [7]

After remaining in front of Camp Bartow for about five hours the

Federal troops were assembled and marched slowly back to Cheat Mountain Fort. If General Reynolds intended to defeat the enemy at Bartow and take possession of the Monterey Pike, his plan failed. If, as his official report claimed, his only objective had been a "forced reconnaissance" of Bartow. Then that at least had been accomplished. It seems odd however, that Reynolds' troops were instructed to carry four days' rations, for a one-day fight.

Back at Cheat Fort the men gathered around to discuss their experiences and write of the battle to friends and loved ones. A member of the 7th Indiana Infantry wrote that he wished he was still at home; "for if I was at home" he said, "I would not come again for nothing in the world. I have wished a thousand times that I had not come."[8]

Rev. W.H. Nickerson of the 32nd Ohio Infantry, preferred to see the positive aspects of their Bartow expedition. He said many of the soldiers were without blankets, shoes, shirts, or even a good pair of pants. He said that on the "day of our battle...I saw a number of men...that had no pants, but who marched in the night to the attack and returned next day with drawers on."[9] [10]

Another member of the 32nd Ohio, Pvt. W.S. Hord, was slightly less honest than his regimental chaplain in his correspondence. Private Hord said that they "had some fun with the mountaineers. We made them a visit and the first introduction they had was a bombshell exploding in their camp. There was 25 thousand of them and nine thousand of us but we made them hoist the flag of truce after half an hours firing...we killed five hundred of them and wounded the same."[11]

Back at Bartow, the victorious Confederates spent Oct. 4th going over the battleground picking up souvenirs and repairing damages. Sgt. S.G. Pryor, from Georgia, told his wife there were "cannon balls and pieces of shell lying all over our camp...the sign of the battle can be seen by looking at our tents, the ball holes through them, some of them literally torn to pieces..." Pryor also claimed the Yankees left one of their regimental flags on the field of battle. He said it was a "very large beautiful flag."[12]

At Sewell Mountain, General Loring announced the victory to his troops on Oct. 7th: "The general commanding has the pleasure to announce to the Army of the Northwest a signal defeat of the enemy from the fortifications of Cheat Mountain by the division of Brigadier-General Jackson. After three attempts of four and a half hours to force our lines in front and on both flanks with a superior force of artillery, some with longer range, he was repulsed with a considerable loss. The general commanding tenders his thanks to Brigadier-General Jackson, his officers and soldiers, for their gallant conduct in this engagement, and assures them that they will have the grateful remembrance of our people. By command of Brigadier-General Loring..."[13]

The author at Bartow in 1982. The convex mound in the foreground is a Confederate cannon emplacement. This view is looking from the heights of the Confederate position toward Cheat Fort. The Federal artillery was placed in the fields to the left center in this photograph. Flank attempts were made by General Reynolds' troops to the left and right. Courtesy Jerry McKinney, Carthage, Ind.

Confederate trench remains can be seen tracing the crown of this hill at Camp Bartow.
This is a 1982 view.

Return of casualties in the Union forces in the engagement on Greenbrier River, West Virginia, October 3, 1861.[†]

Command.	Killed.		Wounded.		Aggregate.
	Officers.	Enlisted men.	Officers.	Enlisted men.	
Seventh Indiana			1	7	8
Ninth Indiana		2		6	8
Thirteenth Indiana		1		1	2
Fourteenth Indiana		1	1	5	7
Seventeenth Indiana		1		3	4
Twenty-fourth Ohio		2		3	5
Twenty-fifth Ohio				3	3
Howe's (Fourth U. S.) battery		1		5	6
Total		8	2	33	43

[*] Not found.   [†] Compiled from records of Adjutant-General's Office.

[Inclosures.]

List of casualties at the battle of Greenbrier River, October 3, 1861.

Command.	Killed.		Wounded.		Missing.		Aggregate.
	Officers.	Enlisted men.	Officers.	Enlisted men.	Officers.	Enlisted men.	
Third Arkansas		2		9		4	15
First Georgia		1		1			2
Twelfth Georgia		1		4			5
Twenty-third Virginia				2			2
Thirty-first Virginia		1	1	2		9	13
Forty-fourth Virginia			1	4			5
Rice's battery		1	1	4			6
Shumaker's battery			1	3			4
Total		6	4	29		13	52

CLINCHING THE 35TH STAR

$\mathcal{F}$rom his temporary camp near present-day Ansted and Hawks Nest State Park, General Rosecrans notified the War Department on Oct. 8th of his retreat from Sewell Mountain: "Withdrawn our forces...on Sunday. Came to Camp Lookout ...without accident. We failed to draw the Rebels out. Our reasons for this movement were want of transportation, want of force, roads almost impassable....Our troops will fall back to the Gauley and get their pay and clothing. Hold a threatening position, and cut off all assault..."[1]

That same day Frances Pierpont, Acting Governor of the Reorganized Government of Virginia, telegraphed Rosecrans saying that 200 Rebels in Calhoun and Wirt County's had killed seven Union men, and were "burning property daily." Governor Peirpont asked that a regiment then stationed in Roane County be sent to quell the disturbance and restore order. He said for provisions the troops could "quarter and feed on the enemy."[2] The situation Pierpont described was not unique in West Virginia. With debate on the statehood movement and the course of the war still raging, there existed a great division of sentiment throughout the northwest. The question of slavery also added to the debate. Would West Virginia seek admission to the Union as a slave or free-state?

Pursuant to instructions from the War Department, General Rosecrans changed the name of his military district to the "Department of Western Virginia," on Oct. 11. His order designated all of Virginia west of the Blue Ridge Mountains as comprising that department.[3]

On Oct. 12, General Lee's plan to advance Floyd's Brigade into the Kanawha Valley was implemented, with Floyd and 5,000 soldiers marching away from Camp Defiance. Over on the Monterey line, at Camp Bartow, General Jackson wrote to the Confederate War Department on the 12th, advising them that the lack of a commissioned quartermaster for his army was damaging the effectiveness of his command. Jackson said his horses were starving and that with winter approaching his situation would become critical unless something was done. This was also the case at Camp Allegheny, a few miles from Bartow, where Col. John Baldwin was in

Federal pickets at Hawks Nest, present-day Ansted, W.Va. and Hawks Nest State Park.
Courtesy Fayette County Historical Society

command. A few days after Jackson's telegraph, Colonel Baldwin notified the War Department of his difficulty in procuring supplies: "...the army on this line cannot depend upon the surrounding country for supplies of any kind....At the best the distance from this point to Petersburg is at least 70 miles...from Staunton, the distance to this point is 60 miles...The road in summer is good, but in winter may fairly be said to be impassable for wagons...a single snow-storm... would starve every horse in this army...and would seriously endanger the entire command....Already the weather has been such as to freeze the tents of my regiment solid after a soaking rain and to coat the water in vessels with thick ice..." Colonel Baldwin added that he would order winter quarters constructed if told to maintain his position.[4]

At Sewell Mountain General Lee was left with approximately 4,000 men. These consisted of Loring's men, part of the Wise Legion, and the 14th North Carolina Infantry. Lee began moving his immediate command to Meadow Bluff within a few days of Floyd's departure. On Oct. 15, Lee wrote to General Floyd advising him that a spy of his had entered the Federal camp at Gauley Bridge. The spy reported the enemy as being 14,000 strong, almost double their actual manpower. Lee also explained why he had not yet assumed the offensive, as he and Floyd had planned: "I should have advanced toward Gauley, had it been possible to take the road...I sent the quartermaster and commissary on the road to see what could be procured and they report literally nothing....the men of the Wise Legion are suffering much for want of clothing. The horses of the command are without provender." Lee also said the situation at his camp was nearly desperate: "We barely get bread from day to day. No forage." In the face of these numerous problems General Lee had determined that the campaign in this area was nearing an end. He had now begun to see that nothing significant could be accomplished in West Virginia before the winter. He could march with few men and fewer supplies toward the Kanawha Valley, or he could assist the movement of provisions to General Floyd and focus his attention elsewhere. He chose the latter.[5]

The next day Lee wrote again to General Floyd, discussing the locations of the enemy generally and telling his subordinate that the occupation of Cotton Hill (a mountain opposite Gauley Bridge) would put his army in position to annoy the enemy. This was merely a suggestion however, with the final decision left to Floyd's discretion: "You must judge of the means at your disposal how you can best operate against them or whether any aid can be given you on this side...General Loring thinks it important for his command to return to his line. The reports from there indicate another attack."[6]

By Oct. 18, the large numbers of sick troops that had been at Camp Defiance were almost entirely gone. Lee sent them to the military hospitals at Lewisburg, White Sulphur Springs, and Blue Sulphur Springs. By Oct. 20, Lee had decided to return to Richmond, ending his direct involvement in the West Virginia campaign. On that date he notified Floyd of his decision. He also explained that military necessity required him to order General Loring's troops back to the Huntersville line: "I must inform you that General Loring has received dispatches tonight from Generals Jackson and Donelson confirmatory of several previous reports indicative of attacks on both of their lines, and calling earnestly for aid. I have resisted these appeals for some time...in the hope of uniting in an attack with your force from the left bank of the Kanawha on General Rosecrans ...I do not think it proper to retain General Loring any longer...and I have not heard what time you expect to make your contemplated movement down the Kanawha...On reaching Meadow Bluff I will inform you of the probable time of my return to Richmond."[7]

Federal troops had been engaged for several days in minor activity in the direction of the Staunton and Virginia Central Railroad, and it would have been improper for Lee to maintain such a large force in an area of inactivity. During the evening of the 20th Lee issued marching orders to General Loring, thanking him sincerely for his assistance, and saying that he regretted the "necessity which calls you from this line..."[8]

Also on Oct. 20, General Jackson wrote from Camp Bartow, complaining about the lack of sufficient manpower on that line to meet the various threats of the enemy. He said they were camped in the immediate presence of a much superior force, and added that he was "lost in astonishment" that the War Department had not seen fit to better prepare a defense of that section.[9]

Events would show that General Jackson was not the only Southern officer astonished at the way the war was conducted. He was joined in that feeling by General Floyd, who was manifestly agitated over Lee's decision to order Loring away and return himself to Richmond.

On Oct. 21, Lee and Loring rode away from Sewell Mountain. General Lee moved the few soldiers remaining at Camp Defiance to Meadow Bluff, where he established temporary headquarters. Also on the 21st, Floyd's army of 5,000 reached Fayetteville, within 10 or 11 miles of General Rosecrans and company.[10]

In the northeast matters were heating-up with the Union garrison at Harpers Ferry attacked on Oct. 16th, by 500 Confederates under Col. Turner Ashby. Though Ashby's men were repulsed the War Department notified General Rosecrans on Oct. 23rd, that Gen. B.F. Kelley had been ordered to leave Grafton and assume command at Harpers Ferry. After

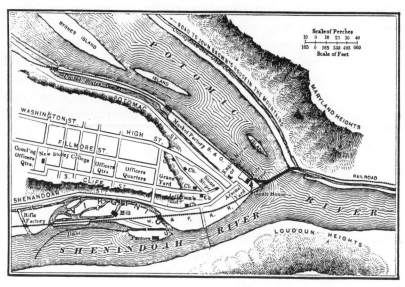

MAP OF HARPER'S FERRY.

arriving there General Kelley issued a proclamation to the "People of Hampshire County and the Upper Potomac." Saying that he was there to assist, and not to destroy the people, Kelley promised fair treatment. "But" he said, "if you attempt to carry on a guerrilla warfare against my troops, by attacking my wagon trains or messengers, or shooting my guards or pickets, you will be considered as enemies of your country, and treated accordingly."[11] [12]

General Floyd moved from Fayetteville to an encampment near the eastern base of Cotton Hill, within easy marching distance of the enemy. On Oct. 27, he sent a less than truthful letter to the Secretary of War. In it, Floyd said he had accomplished his assigned objectives thus far, but that he had not heard from General Lee.[13] Of course this claim was false, as Lee had advised General Floyd on the 20th that he was sending Loring away, that he anticipated returning to Richmond, and that his camp would now be at Meadow Bluff.

Adding arrogance to lies, Floyd wrote to Lee on the 28th, saying he had artillery on the heights overlooking the enemy at Gauley Bridge, and adding that if Lee would now advance from Sewell Mountain into the Kanawha Valley, they might exterminate the enemy.[14]

General Lee must have found the ex-governor's message puzzling. He replied that he had already advised Floyd of Loring's departure, and that he would be leaving for Richmond that day (the 29th). He explained further that Col. James L. Davis was in command of the troops remaining at Meadow Bluff.[15]

There is of course no way to determine the motive for General Floyd's obvious attempt at deceit. He lied to the Secretary of War, and attempted to alter Lee's stated plans by acting as though he had no prior knowledge of them. It may be that he was so desperate for victory in West Virginia that his temperament could not accept the inevitable. Perhaps Floyd felt that he could manipulate General Lee into remaining in the region until the question of possession was more firmly established. Lee, of course, being a military man by training, did not need any additional confirmation of the obvious. His aide, Colonel Taylor, described the situation well: "...the lateness of the season and the condition of the roads precluded the idea of earnest aggressive operations, and the campaign...was virtually concluded....At its conclusion a large portion of the state was in possession of the Federals...For this, however, General Lee cannot be reasonably held accountable....the worst had been accomplished, before he reached the theatre of operations..."[16]

Lee's departure did indeed signal the loss of West Virginia from the Confederacy. On Oct. 24, a majority of those who voted, overwhelmingly approved the new-state plan. General Lee and Colonel Taylor reached Richmond on the 31st of October. Their absence did not however, signal

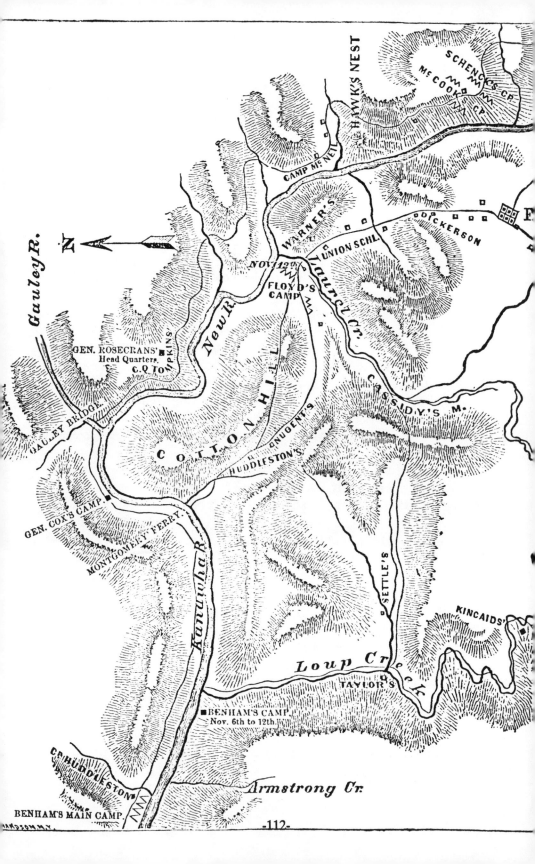

N

Gauley R.

SCHENCK'S CR.

HAWK'S NEST

MC COOK'S CR.

CAMP MC NEIL

WARNER'S

DICKERSON

UNION SCHL

Laurel Cr.

NOV 12

FLOYD'S CAMP

New R.

GEN. ROSECRANS'
Head Quarters.
C.Q TOMPKINS'

CASSIDY'S M.

NUGENT'S

C O T T O N   H I L L

GAULEY BRIDGE

HUDDLESTON'S

GEN. COX'S CAMP.

MONTGOMERY FERRY

SETTLE'S

Kanawha R.

KINCAIDS'

Loup Creek

TAYLOR'S

BENHAM'S CAMP.
Nov. 6th to 12th.

CP. HUDDLESTON

Armstrong Cr.

BENHAM'S MAIN CAMP.

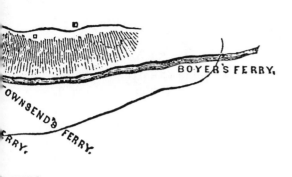

BOYER'S FERRY,

OWNSEND'S FERRY.

ERRY,

VILLE

HAWKIN'S

✝ *NOV. 14*

CROGHAN. KP

NOV. 11th

Mc COY'S M.

S M.

Big Loup Cr.

TO PAINT CR.

BLAKE'S or KETON'S

TO PAINT

NOTE.

From Loup Creek Mouth to Fayetteville, by Hud-
dlestone's, ... 15 miles.
From Fayetteville to Blake's, ... 15 "

.*. *Crossed swords denote skirmishes.*

the end of the 1861 military activity in West Virginia. General Floyd remained on the Kanawha line for two more weeks. On Nov. 1st, he opened fire with artillery from the heights of Cotton Hill into the Yankee camps at and near Gauley Bridge. This was more a harassing action than a serious threat to Federal control in the area, and after an artillery duel which continued for six days, Floyd's guns were silenced. He was driven completely out of the area in a series of skirmishes which began on Nov. 10. By the 14th, there were no Confederate forces west of Meadow Bluff. Floyd's Brigade continued their retreat all the way south to the security of Dublin Depot, Virginia, on the Virginia and Tennessee Railroad. After a rest and reorganization, Floyd's Brigade, with the exception of the 22nd Virginia Infantry, was transferred to Bowling Green, Kentucky, to serve under Gen. Albert Sidney Johnston.[17]

With Floyd's defeat several regiments under General Rosecrans' command were also sent into Kentucky, and the remainder began preparing winter quarters. Over on the Huntersville and Monterey lines, troops on both sides of the conflict were also preparing their winter quarters and trying to acquire sufficient supplies for what promised to be a long, frigid winter.

During the second and third weeks of November detachments of Union troops were sent from Cheat Summit Fort in the direction of Bartow. Their mission was to capture some cattle known to be in the valley, and, if possible, determine the activity's of the enemy. These excursions resulted in a number of insignificant skirmishes in the vicinity of Camp Bartow.[18]

A veteran of the 1st Georgia Infantry, part of General Jackson's command, described what a snow storm was like before their log huts had been completed: "The snow had fallen during the night to the depth of eight inches, and it was a strange sight to see the whole camp snowed under ... When morning approached, the writer while not asleep, was not entirely aroused. He lay there under his blanket, a gentle perspiration was oozing from every pore of his skin, when suddenly, he aroused himself, and rose up. Not a man was to be seen, the hillocks of snow, however, showed where they lay, so I hollored, 'look at the snow.' Like jumping out of the graves, the men pounced up in a jiffy, they were wrestling and snowballing and rubbing each other with it..."[19]

It was an altogether different matter later on, when troops at Camp Allegheny were housed in new log huts. A member of the 12th Georgia Infantry told his sister about their humble dwellings on Nov. 28th: "Well sis we are into winter quarters at last...16 men crowded into one little hut−16ft by 16ft−one small fireplace to cook, eat, and warm around, and the weather cold, bitter cold, snow all over the ground, and a difficult matter to get wood...Today we are going to commence building fortifica-

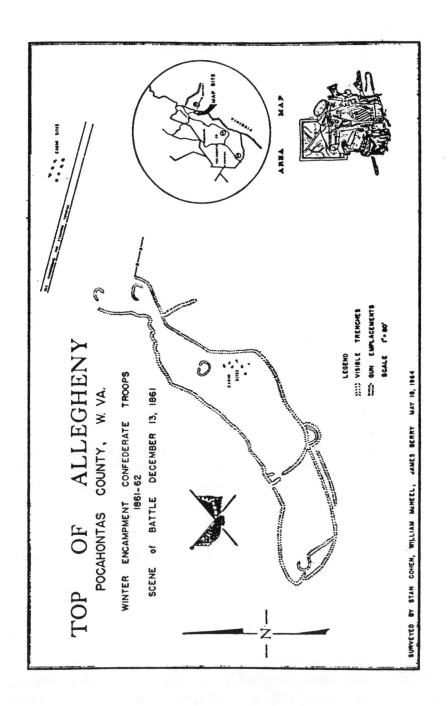

TOP OF ALLEGHENY

POCAHONTAS COUNTY, W. VA.

WINTER ENCAMPMENT CONFEDERATE TROOPS
1861-62

SCENE of BATTLE DECEMBER 13, 1861

LEGEND

VISIBLE TRENCHES

GUN EMPLACEMENTS

SCALE 1"= 80'

SURVEYED BY STAN COHEN, WILLIAM McNEEL, JAMES BERRY MAY 18, 1964

ARMA MAP

MAP SITE

VIRGINIA

CAMP SITES

N

tions and entrenching the whole camp; think of all this and ten thousand other things too tedious to mention that tend to render an individual miserable, and you will have a faint idea of the true condition of a soldier in this portion of Virginia."[20]

On Nov. 21, General Jackson evacuated Camp Bartow and retired to the summit of Allegheny Mountain, leaving a token cavalry detachment at Bartow to watch the enemy. On the 22nd, he ordered Col. Edward Johnson, of the 12th Georgia Infantry, to assume command of the garrison at the summit. This force consisted of the 12th Georgia, the 25th, 31st, and 52nd Virginia Infantry Regiment's, the 9th Battalion Virginia Infantry, a company of cavalry, and two artillery batteries. The 44th Virginia Infantry and another artillery battery, located on the road to Monterey, were added to his command. At this time Monterey was occupied by the 1st Georgia Infantry, the 3rd Arkansas, the 23rd and 37th Virginia Infantry Regiment's, with cavalry, and orders to patrol down the branches of the Potomac River toward Petersburg and Moorefield.

Acting on orders from Gen. Robert H. Milroy, a Federal force of 1,760 men left Cheat Fort to attack Camp Allegheny (or Camp Baldwin) on Dec. 12. Advancing near Camp Bartow these men were met on the afternoon of the 12th by a 106-man scouting party from Camp Allegheny. The Confederate scouts clashed briefly with the advance of the enemy, retiring that night to Camp Allegheny and advising Col. Edward Johnson of the enemy approach. Of Colonel Johnson's force on the mountain only about 1,200 were effective. General Milroy's men were divided into two attacking columns; sent through the woods to fall on the enemy's right and rear was a detachment of 830 men, with the remainder sent directly up the Monterey Pike to attack the enemy in front and on their left.

At 4:00 a.m. of the 13th desultory firing began between Confederate pickets and advance elements of Milroy's force. At 7:15 a.m. the column sent to attack the right of Camp Allegheny reached their assigned position and the battle began in earnest. The Federal assault was intended to be carried out on the left and right simultaneously but this failed to develop. Colonel Johnson was able to detach part of his force from the left to the right, in all about 500 men on the right. These men met the bloody assaults of the Yankees until early afternoon in a series of engagements which were at times nearly hand to hand. Milroy's soldiers then retreated from the mountain, gathering their wounded but leaving their dead on the field. About one-half hour after the fighting on the right ceased, Milroy's force sent to the left made their attack. This, too, resulted in heavy fighting and considerable death and injury to both sides. Johnson's left had been entrenched, whereas his right had not at the time of the battle. His men fought gallantly holding their position against a number of bold enemy assaults. Colonel Johnson ordered his men on the right to move over to the left, and this increased force succeeded in repulsing the Yankees, driving them down the mountain. For this victory Colonel Johnson was promoted to Brigadier-General. He also acquired the nickname "Allegheny Johnson."[21]

In his official report Johnson said the Yankees were led in their assault by two local men who were familiar with the area. He also said the enemy was known to be very much demoralized by the defeat: "The enemy was totally routed. I hear from citizens on the line of their retreat that they carried numbers of dead and wounded by the houses, and acknowledged they had been badly whipped....They were much demoralized, and I hope they have received a good lesson."

Upon reaching the scene of their fight with the scouting party the previous day, the retreating Yankees observed the bodies of their fallen comrades. If the gruesome scene on the mountain was not a "lesson" then this probably was. Ambrose Bierce, of the 9th Indiana Infantry, described what they saw: "Repassing the spot the next day, a beaten, despirited and exhausted force, feeble from fatigue and savage from defeat, some of us had life enough left, such as it was, to observe that these bodies had altered their positions. They appeared also to have thrown off some of their clothing, which lay near by, in disorder. Their expression, too, had an added blankness—they had no faces....a herd of galloping swine...had eaten our fallen..."[22]

There was some activity on the Kanawha line as well. On Dec. 15, a 150-man Union raiding party went to Meadow Bluff and destroyed 110 log huts which the absent Confederates had intended to use for the winter. They also captured two noted guerrillas, 21 rifles and guns, 21 mules and horses, 95 cattle, and 200 sheep. They skirmished briefly with a few enemy cavalry and returned on Dec. 21st.

The West Virginia campaigns of 1861 were now over. General Rosecrans moved his headquarters to Wheeling during December. General Loring was active at Staunton, working in conjunction with Gen. Stonewall Jackson for a planned attack on Romney. General Reynolds was superseded in command by General Milroy. General Lee was sent during November to supervise the construction of defensive works in South Carolina.

What then, can be said about the tumultuous events of 1861 which ultimately led to the birth of West Virginia, the 35th Star on our nations flag. There can be no doubt that General Lee and others in roles of leadership for the Confederacy, seriously, fatally, miscalculated both the Federal Government's resolve to hold West Virgina, and the strong division of sentiment among its populace. From the earliest days of the conflict it may be fairly stated that the South's attempts to retain West Virginia were feeble at best. Even if the weather had not been as it was, it is doubtful, given the slow and inadequate reactions of the Confederates, that they would have accomplished much more in this state than they did. From the outset their efforts were plagued on several fronts by the inept work of politicians, who knew nothing of warfare. On the positive side, they were able to prevent the Federal forces from advancing east of the Blue Ridge Mountains, or south of Lewisburg. Had the Northern army done either in force, it would have spelled disaster for the Confederacy very early in the conflict.

The Northern forces were not entirely successful either. They were, perhaps, more the beneficiaries of an initially inept enemy, than the heroes of a successful campaign. General Rosecrans had begun the campaign in July with the announced purpose of marching to Wytheville, Virginia, and on into the Holston Valley. General McClellan had cherished the idea of making the Kanawha line the base of operations into the same region. It was easy to sweep a hand over a few inches of map, showing nothing of the topography, and to say, "We will march from here to here." The almost wilderness nature of the country, with its weary miles of steep mountain roads that became impassable in wet weather, and the acute absence of forage for animals, were elements which the Federal commanders greatly underestimated.

The spectacular campaigns of the Army of the Potomac in the East and of General Grant in the West, relegated the West Virginia campaigns of 1861 into obscurity. The Southern Confederacy lost the mineral resources (especially salt) of the Kanawha region. The Baltimore and Ohio Railroad, referred to by historian Festus Summers as "Lincoln's lifeline," remained in Federal control. More than that, a new state appeared on the horizon. On March 26, 1863, the Willey Amendment was ratified by the people of the new state. This amendment provided for gradual abolition of slavery. On June 20, 1863, West Virginia was admitted to the Union. In response to that fact the colorful and ever combative Gen. Henry A. Wise declared that the new state was the "bastard offspring of political rape."

Return of casualties in the Union forces in the engagement at Camp Alleghany, W. Va., December 13, 1861.

Command.	Killed.	Wounded.	Missing.	Aggregate.
Ninth Indiana	8	13	......	21
Thirteenth Indiana	2	23	4	29
Twenty-fifth Ohio	6	54	6	66
Thirty-second Ohio	2	10	......	12
Second West Virginia	2	7	......	9
Total	20	107	10	137

Return of casualties in Colonel Edward Johnson's command in the engagement at Camp Alleghany, December 13, 1861. *

Command.	Killed.		Wounded.		Missing.		Aggregate.
	Officers.	Enlisted men.	Officers.	Enlisted men.	Officers.	Enlisted men.	
Brigade staff	......	......	2	......	......	......	2
Twelfth Georgia	1	5	1	36	......	4	47
Twenty-fifth Virginia	1	1	......	11	......	5	18
Thirty-first Virginia	1	5	4	27	......	......	37
Fifty-second Virginia	......	......	......	2	......	6	8
Hansbrough's battalion	1	3	1	10	......	13	28
Lee Battery	1	......	......	......	......	......	1
Miller's battery	......	1	1	3	......	......	5
Totals	5	15	9	89	......	28	146

APPENDIX A

The following is from a Confederate Veteran's letter which was published
in the *Pocahontas Times*, Marlinton, W.Va., July 5, 1895.
It is included here courtesy of Bill McNeel, Marlinton, W.Va.

I leisurely started up Valley Mountain in Pocahontas County, where I now write this letter. Age has taken from me the agility and strength that were mine in those memorable days when under the glorious Lee I learned here the rudiments of war. But age has not, thank God! deprived me of memory. How vividly comes back the scenes of 1861. Here among the sublime mountains patriotic men came to learn their first lesson in practical duty. Every glen and ravine, every road and by-path are vividly plain and tenderly remembered. The camp-ground of the several regiments, Lee's headquarters I can plainly locate, and the dead- the dear, honored dead rise and stand before me on the tented field of memory.

Sitting on a log close to my old quarters, I lovingly but sadly recall the past. Every spot around me has a tender memory attached to it, and incidents I long thought lost among buried dreams, come back in fresh reality to my mind. Where now are the noble fellows whose joys and sorrows I shared here in the early days of our struggle? Many lie in gory graves, and few I know who came out of the conflict now living. Here around our bivouac fires fond hearts poured forth in songs- sweet old home songs- the sweetest and saddest effusions of love. Anecdote and joke went freely round each happy circle, and no gloomy anticipations cast a shadow on our happy, cheerful minds. In the ranks manhood asserted its claim to the highest order of heroism.

I remember Lee in that springtime of his military fame. Physically, he was grand; morally, he was magnificent. How calm and majestic, how graceful and gentle. He was in all that the word implies a gentleman. No artificial honors were needed to add to his natural dignity. He was a soldier and a christian, and duty was the highest principle he cherished as either. Many an ardent young man panting for fame felt the influence of Lee's patient, gentle example. It was a pleasure to me to look at him occasionally. It was an honor to serve under such a man.

And here it was that Lee's first army encamped. Where is that army now? Nearly all on the camping ground of eternity, and I, the least of rank and file, sit here a worn-out, solitary veteran, holding a love-feast in the temple of memory, with the gallant chivalry of the South's fallen cause.

There was more in the fruitless campaign of 1861, in Pocahontas County, W.Va., than many person could have thought. Here Virginians were at home, also Tennesseeans, North Carolinians, South Carolinians, Georgians, and others. The climate was severe on those from the farther South, and the season was unusually wet and disagreeable. Climatic changes were to be overcome, hardness to be endured as a necessary discipline, and obedience sternly inculcated. Add to all this men of different States, of different manners, customs, and ideas were to be brought together. Under the mild government of General Lee all these differences gave way to a noble, generous spirit of brotherly love.

I reluctantly leave the past and apply myself to the present. The Confederate veterans of Pocahontas County have organized an encampment, at the head of which is Colonel Gatewood....This encampment has one grand object at present in view. It is the burial of all the Confederates who dies in Pocahontas in one neat cemetery at or close to Marlinton on the beautiful Greenbrier River....Where there is no respect paid the heroic dead- where there is no pantheon in which to enshrine their sacred dust and their glorious memory, civilization is at a low ebb and manhood is degraded.

West Virginia is nobly coming forward to join her sister States of the South in preserving the memory of her Confederate dead, and inspiring the living with faith, hope, and charity....The mementoes of our struggle are too valuable to be lost by neglect or callous apathy. Clustering around every battle-field won or lost by us are traditional stones which it were a crime to let die away, and deeds of heroism one can claim before the world, which it is our duty to keep fresh...The roll of our fame shall be preserved and the records of our struggle enshrined in the holiest crypt of memory. There is nothing sectional in love- nothing treasonable in duty.

Let it not be forgotten that a Confederate Veteran Encampment is incomplete without the "Daughters of the Confederacy." The women of the South cannot be deprived of the glory so nobly won by them during the war of the States....

The sun is going down the western slopes amid gorgeous clouds in splendid serenity. So went down many a noble cause, but the sun will rise again. In the cool of evening I leave for Marlinton. Adieu, dear old Valley Mountain.

C.P.K.

(The author has been unable to determine who C.P.K. was.)

APPENDIX B

The recollections of Mr. A.S. Horsley, veteran of the 1st Tennessee Infantry, 1861.
Originally published in the *Pocahontas Times*, Marlinton, W.Va., Feb. 7, 1896.
It is included here courtesy of Bill McNeel, Marlinton, W.Va.

During the past summer and fall I passed over roads that the First Tennessee Regiment went over from August to December, 1861, in Greenbrier, Pocahontas, Randolph and Battle counties. I walked to the spot where General Lee's tent stood on Valley Mountain, and from a point near which I could see Mingo Flats and Cheat Mountain, along whose great sides we clambered for several days, and where we had our first fight or skirmish on the summit, in a blackberry patch. I would also see where old Colonel John H. Savage marched along in a deep valley, and captured thirty Yankees by himself one foggy morning, Sept. 11, 1861. They were in a house, and their guns were stacked outside. His men had captured the Vidette, and he rushed ahead of the advance guard and, getting between the Yankees and their guns - made them surrender.

The Valley Mountain country has greatly changed, an English colony having bought it and cleared off the timber and made stock farms. It is a fine bluegrass country. At Big Springs I found our old camp, through Major Cam. Gatewood, who pointed out the cold spring, from which I drank after an absence of over thirty-four years. A stonehouse stands where our regiment camped. There a big white frost fell in August, and one of the company (Jack Butler's captain) accidently discharged his gun while cleaning up for Sunday's inspection, and it killed one of Colonel Hatton's men, of the Seventh. I saw his grave on the hill in a grove of locust trees. I remember well his burial with military honors, the band playing Pleyel's Hymn, or funeral march. Sitting here by the cold spring I could also see in the distance up the creek and valley a tree which Captain Hume R. Field - afterwards colonel - used to shoot against with his Colt's repeating rifle, with which gun he killed and wounded half a dozen Yankees while on a scouting expedition with Lieutenant Randolph.

I followed the trail of our regiment 140 miles and stopped at all our old camps. The decades had made many changes.

I have read with much interest Brom Ridley's narrative. Some mistakes occur, one of which is where he says Lovejoy Station is where President Davis visited the Army of Tennessee. "Palmetto" is the station. I went three miles to hear Mr. Davis and Howell Cobb speak. Mr. Davis was a charming speaker, and impressive. But General Cobb was more impassioned. He was a large, fleshy man, while Mr. Davis was of the Cassius sort - lean. In a few days we started on the unfortunate campaign into Middle Tennessee, which resulted so unfortunately.

While at Meadow Bluff last summer I saw the spot where we camped on our return from Sewell Mountain. We put up our tents during a rain, or water spout, and Corporals Phifer and Schwartz, of Captain Harsch's company had a terrific fist fight during the heaviest part of the rain. Schwartz had stolen Phifer's ten-pound tallow cake out of his knapsack and replaced it with a fifteen-pound rock, which Phifer carried all day. I was also reminded at Meadow Bluff of an eighteen-mile foot-race Billy Whitthorne ran between Meadow Bluff and Lewisburg. This is now West Virginia.

FOOTNOTES

Chapter One

1. Allan Pinkertonn, *Spy of the Rebellion*. New York: 1883.
2. *Journal of the Senate of the Commonwealth of Virginia, 1861, Extra Session*. Rich mond, Va.: 1861, pg. 3.
3. *The Wheeling Intelligencer*, February 4, 1861.
4. Richard Orr Curry, *A House Divided....* University of Pittsburg Press, Pittsburg, Penna.: 1964, pg. 53.
5. James C. Linger, *Confederate Military Units of West Virginia*. Privately printed, Tulsa, Okla.: 1992. (This is a work in progress. The author's conclusions are based on substantial new research and documentation.)
6. *The Wheeling Intelligencer*, April 26, 1861.
7. *Official Records*, V. 2, pg. 788.
8. *Ibid.*
9. Theodore F. Lang, *Loyal West Virginia From 1861-1865*. Deutch Pub. Co., Baltimore, Md.: 1895, pg. 23
10. *Ibid.*, pg. 24
11. *Ibid.*, pg. 25
12. *Ibid.*
13. For additional detail see Curry, *A House Divided*, pgs. 38 to 45.
14. *Official Records*, V. 2, pg. 48
15. Curry, *A House Divided*, pg. 56
16. Though the claim is often disputed, the fight at Philippi is generally referred to as the first land battle of the war.
17. Curry, *A House Divided*, pg. 57
18. *Official Records*, V. 2, pgs. 236-38
19. *Ibid.*, pg. 237
20. George B. McClellan, *McClellan's Own Story*, New York: 1887, pg. 57.
21. George B. McClellan, *Report on the Organization and Campaigns of the Army of the Potomac to which is added an account of the Campaign in Western Virginia*, New York: 1864, pgs. 22-23.
22. John S. Wise, *End of an Era*, A.S. Barnes & Co., New York: 1965, pg. 177.
23. "Memoir of a Youthful Confederate," *Jackson County Miscellany*, Jackson Co. West Virginia Historical Society.
24. Situated about midway between Parkersburg and Charleston, Ripley was a strategically important community early in the conflict. The area witnessed

numerous skirmishes and troop movements during the war years.

25. W.C. Clark, "The Journal of a Soldier of 1861," *West Virginia Review*, November, 1930.

26. From the papers of the C.Q. Tompkins family in the manuscript collections of the Virginia Historical Society Richmond, Va.

27. *Official Records*, V. 2, pgs. 243-44.

28. Boyd Stutler, *The Civil War in West Virginia*, Education Foundation, Inc., Charleston, W.Va.: 1863, pg. 67.

29. Terry Lowry, *The Battle of Scary Creek*, Pictorial Histories Pub. Co., Charleston, W.Va.: 1982, pg. 162

30. *Official Records*, V. 2, pg. 1012.

31. Fritz Haselberger, *Yanks From the South!...*, Past Glories Press, Baltimore, Md.: 1987.

32. Lang, *Loyal West Virginia From 1861 to 1865*, pg. 41.

33. Stephen D. Engle, *Thunder in the Hills*, Mountain State Press, University of Charleston, W.Va.: 1989, pgs. 9-10 and "Appendix 1," pg. 94.

34. Otis K. Rice, *West Virginia The State and Its People*, McClain Printing Co., Parsons, W.Va.: 1972, pgs. 170-72.

Chapter Two

1. *Official Records*, V. 5, pg. 552. (General Orders #7).

2. *Ibid.*

3. *Ibid.*, pg. 553

4. *Ibid.*, pgs. 554-55.

5. *Ibid.*

6. *Official Records*, V. 51, pt. 1, pgs. 444-45.

7. *Official Records*, V. 5, pg. 554.

8. *Ibid.*, pgs. 555-56.

Chapter Three

1. Clement A. Evans, ed., *Confederate Military History*, Confederate Pub. Co., Atlanta, Ga.: 1899, V. 3, pg. 153.

2. William T. Price, *Historical Sketches of Pocahontas County West Virginia*, Price Brothers Pub., Marlinton, W.Va.: 1901, pg. 597.

3. Charles T. Quintard, *Dr. Quintard: Chaplain C.S.A. and Second Bishop of Tennessee*, A.H. Noll, ed.: 1905, pg. 17.

4. Walter H. Taylor. *General Lee His Campaigns in Virginia 1861 to 1865*, (reprint) Morningside Bookshop. Dayton, Ohio,: 1975, pgs. 27-8.

5. James V. Drake, *Life of General Robert Hatton...*, Marshall and Bruce, Nashville, Tenn.: 1867, pgs. 366-67.

6. Oliver Taylor, "The War Story of a Confederate Soldier Boy," (37th Va. Infantry) as published in the Bristol, Tenn. *Herald-Courier*, between Jan. 23 and Feb. 27, 1921.

7. Drake, *Life of General Robert Hatton*, pgs. 368-69

8. Marcus B. Toney, *The Privations of a Private*, Privately printed, Nashville, Tenn.:

1905, pg. 19.

9. *Official Records*, V. 2, pgs. 981.

10. *Ibid.*, V. 51, pt. 2, pg. 206.

11. *Ibid.*, pgs. 210.

12. *Ibid.*, pg. 211.

13. *Ibid.*, V. 5, pg. 768.

14. *Ibid.*, V. 51, pt. 2, pg. 211.

15. *Ibid.*, V. 5, pg. 773.

16. Robert E. Lee Jr., *Recollections and Letters of Gen. Robert E. Lee*, New York: 1904, pgs. 38-39.

17. *Official Records*, V. 5, pgs. 771-72.

18. *Ibid.*, pg. 773.

19. *Ibid.*

20. Eva Margaret Carnes, "George W. Peterkin at Valley Mountain," *Randolph Co. Historical Society Magazine of History and Biography*, V. 12: 1961.

21. Sam R. Watkins, *Co. Aytch Maury Grays, First Tennessee Regiment*, Cumberland Presbyterian Pub. House, Nashville, Tenn.: 1882, pg. 19.

22. *Official Records*, V. 5, pg. 774.

Chapter Four

1. John H. Worsham, *One of Jackson's Foot Cavalry*, McCowat-Mercer Press, Jackson, Tenn.: 1964, pg. 15. (James I. Robertson Jr., ed.).

2. B.H. Cathey, "Additional Sketch Sixteenth Regiment," (North Carolina Infantry) in *Histories and Battalions From North Carolina in the Great War, 1861-65*, Walter Clark, ed., V. 4, pg. 753.

3. James V. Drake, *Life of General Robert Hatton...*, Marshall and Bruce, Nashville, Tenn.: 1867, pg. 372.

4. Calvin L. Collier, *They'll Do To Tie To! The Story of the Third Regiment Arkansas Infantry C.S.A.*, Pioneer Press, Little Rock, Ark.: 1959, pg. 37.

5. From the Prior Family Papers, Tulip Ark., in the manuscript collections of the University of Arkansas Libraries, Fayetteville, Ark. (3rd Arkansas Infantry).

6. Elizabeth Paisley Huckaby and Ethel C. Simpson, editors, *Tulip Evermore: Emma Butler and William Paisley Their Lives in Letters, 1857-1887*, University of Arkansas Press, Fayetteville, Ark.: 1985, pg. 26.

7. Paul E. Steiner, *Disease in the Civil War: Biological Warfare in 1861-65*, Springfield, Ill.: 1968, pgs. 53-64.

8. Walter H. Taylor, *Four Years With General Lee*, Indiana University Press reprint: 1962, pg. 17.

Chapter Five

1. Robert E. Lee Jr., *Recollections and Letters of Gen. Robert E. Lee*, New York: 1904, pg. 39.

2. From a soldier's letter dated Aug. 7, 1861, at Huttonsville, Va., and published in the *Indianapolis Journal*, Aug. 14, 1861.

3. *Ibid.*, unsigned letter dated Aug. 1, 1861, at Foot of Cheat Mountain, Va.

4. *Ibid.*, from a member of the 15th Indiana Infantry. Letter dated Aug. 28, 1861, at Cheat Mountain, Va.

5. Catherine Merrill, *The Soldier of Indiana in the War for the Union*, Merrill and Company, Indianapolis, Ind.: 1866, pgs. 78-9.

6. Barbara A. Smith, ed., *The Civil War Letters of Col. Elijah H.C. Cabins, 14th Indiana*, Cook-McDowell Publications, Owensboro, Ky.: 1981, pg. 7. These letters were compiled from the originals which are included in the manuscript collections of the Indiana Historical Society, Indianapolis, Ind.)

7. *Official Records*, V. 5, pgs. 561-62.

8. *Ibid.*, pg. 564.

9. *Ibid.*, pgs. 575-77.

10. *Ibid.*, pg. 781.

11. *Ibid.*, pg. 785.

12. *Ibid.*, V. 51, pt. 2, pg. 232.

13. *Ibid.*, B. 5, pg. 156.

14. *Ibid.*, V. 51, pt. 2, pg. 248.

15. *Ibid.*, V. 5, pg. 804.

16. *Ibid.*, pg. 810.

17. Tim McKinney, *The Civil War In Fayette County West Virginia*, Pictorial Histories Pub. Co., Charleston, W.Va.: 1988, pg. 46.

18. Terry Lowry, *September Blood: The Battle of Carnifex Ferry*, Pictorial Histories Pub. Co., Charleston W.Va.: 1985, pg. 28.

19. *Official Records*, V. 5, pg. 117.

20. *Ibid.*, V. 51, pt. 2, pgs. 256-57.

21. *Ibid.*, pg. 264.

Chapter Six

1. *Official Records*, V. 5, pg. 159.

2. Tim McKinney, *The Civil War In Fayette County West Virginia*, Pictorial Histories Pub. Co., Charleston, W.Va.: 1988, pg. 56.

3. *Official Records*, V. 51, pt. 2, pgs. 267-68.

4. *Ibid.*, V. 5, pg. 828.

5. *Ibid.*, V.51, pt. 2, pg. 270.

6. *Ibid.*, V. 5, pg. 586.

7. *Ibid.*, V. 51, pt. 1, pg. 475.

8. *Ibid.*, V. 5, pg. 837.

9. *Ibid.*, pg. 839.

10. *Ibid.*, V. 51, pt. 2, pg. 286.

11. *Ibid.*, V. 5, pg. 838.

12. *Ibid.*, pg. 842.

13. From the papers of Capt. Robert W. Snead, in the manuscript collections of the Virginia Historical Society, Richmond, Va., letter of Sept. 10, 1861.

14. Terry Lowry, *September Blood: The Battle of Carnifex Ferry*, Pictorial Histories Pub. Co., Charleston, W.Va.: 1985.

15. Whitelaw Reid and James G. Smart, ed., *A Radical View: The "Agate" Dispatches of Whitelaw Reid 1861-1865*, Memphis State University Press, Memphis, Tenn.:

1976, pgs. 43-59.

16. *Official Records*, V. 5, pg. 146.

17. *Ibid.*, pg. 848.

18. *Ibid.*, pg. 850.

19. *Ibid.*, pgs. 149-163.

20. During the war years there were several spellings of Carnifex Ferry utilized. The author has used Carnifax Ferry, as that was the way most of the combatants referred to the site in their correspondence.

Chapter Seven

1. Nancy N. Baxter, *Gallant Fourteenth: The Story of an Indiana Civil War Regiment*, The Guild Press, Indianapolis, Ind.: 1980, (paperback edition 1986), pg. 50.

2. From the journal of George Washington Lamber, in the manuscript collections of the Indiana Historical Society, Indianapolis, Ind.

3. Nancy N. Baxter, ed., *Hoosier Farmboy in Lincoln's Army: The Civil War Letters of John R. McClure*, Privately printed: 1969. Quoting McClure's letter of Sept. 18, 1861 to his sister.

4. J.T. Pool, *Under Canvass; or, Recollections of the Fall and Summer Campaign of hte 14th Regiment, Indiana Volunteers*, pgs. 24-5.

5. Robert E. Lee Jr., *Recollections and Letters of Gen. Robert E. Lee*, New York; 1904, pg. 43.

6. Clifford, Dowdey and Louis H. Manarin, editors, *The Wartime Papers of Robert E. Lee*, paperback reprint, Da Capo Press, New York: 1987, pgs. 69-70.

7. C.G. Chamberlayne, ed., *Ham Chamberlayne- Virginian: Letters and Papers of an Artillery Officer*, The Deitz Printing Co., Richmond, Va.: 1932, pg. 34.

8. From the diary of Mary Fontaine; manuscript collections of the University of Charleston, W.Va. Copy courtesy of the Mountain State Press and Dr. Otis K. Rice.

9. From the papers of Richard N. Hewitt, 42nd Va. Infantry, in the manuscript collections of Duke University, Durham, N.C.

10. John A. Cutchins, *A Famous Command: The Richmond Light Infantry Blues*, Garrett & Massie Publishers, Richmond, Va.: 1934, pgs. 88-9.

11. From *Confederate Veteran Magazine*, August 1926, pg. 290.

12. Albert B. Tavel, *Cheat Mountain; or, Unwritten Chapter of the Late War*, A.B. Tavel, Printer, Nashville, Tenn.: 1885, pg. 46.

13. Walter Womack, ed., *The Civil War Diary of Captain J.J. Womack, Co. E. 16th Tennessee Volunteers*, Womack Printing Co., McMinnville, Tenn.: 1961, pg. 14.

14. *Official Records*, V. 5, pg. 192 and V. 51, pt. 2, pg. 283.

15. *Ibid.*, V. 51, pt. 2, pg. 284.

16. *Ibid.*, pg. 285.

17. Thomas A. Head, *Campaigns and Battles of the 16th Regiment Tennessee Volunteers*, Cumberland Presbyterian Publishing House, Nashville, Tenn.: 1885, pg. 32.

18. From the diary of Carroll Clark, 16th Tennessee Inf., in the manuscript collections of the Tennessee State Archives, Nashville, Tenn.

19. Douglas S. Freeman, *R.E. Lee: A Biography*, (4 vols.), New York: 1934-35, V. 1, pgs. 567-68.

20. John Henry Cammack, *Personal Recollections of Private John Henry Cammack: A Soldier of the Confederacy 1861-1865*, Paragon Printing Co., Huntington, W.Va.: 1920, pgs. 35-38.

21. From the papers of William F. Harrison, in the manuscript collections of Duke University, Durham, N.C.

22. A.C. Jones, "The Mountain Campaign Failure," *Confederate Veteran Magazine*: V. 22, pg. 305 and pg. 368.

23. From an unsigned letter to the *Atlanta Confederacy* by a member of the 1st Georgia Infantry, Sept. 18, 1861 at Camp Bartow, Va. As published Sept. 27, 1861 in the *Richmond Dispatch*.

24. *Official Records*, V. 5, pg. 193.

25. *Ibid.*, V. 51, pt. 2, pg. 295.

26. John Levering, "Lee's Advance and Retreat in the Cheat Mountain Campaign in 1861...." From a paper read before the Commandery of the State of Illinois, Military Order of the Loyal Legion of hte United States, Dec. 12, 1889. Published in *Military Essays and Recollections*, V. 4, Cozzens & Beaton Co.: 1907, pgs. 11-35 (pg. 33 cited).

27. Joseph Warren Keifer, *Slavery and Four Years of War*, G.P. Putnam's Sons, New York and London: 1900. Additional Washington family history was obtained from an article which appeared in *Confederate Veteran Magazine*, March 1926, pg. 96.

28. From the papers of John Halvey, included in the manuscript collections of the Indiana Historical Society, Indianapolis, Ind., letter of Sept. 22, 1861.

29. *Confederate Veteran Magazine*, March 1926, pg. 96 and *United Daughters of the Confederacy Magazine*, March 1991, pg. 14.

30. Robert E. Lee Jr., *Recollections and Letters of Gen. Robert E. Lee*, New York: 1904, pgs. 44-46.

31. Freeman, *R.E. Lee: A Biography*, V. 1, pg. 576.

Chapter Eight

1. Jacob D. Cox, *Military Reminiscences*, Charles Scribner & Sons, New York; 1900, pg. 109.

2. *Official Records*, V. 51, pt. 2, pg. 299.

3. *Ibid.*, V. 5, pg. 853.

4. *Ibid.*, pgs. 854-55.

5. From the papers of Lieut. D.B. Baldwin, in the manuscript collections of the Virginia Historical Society, Richmond, Va., letter of Sept. 18, 1861.

6. *Official Records*, V. 51, pt. 1, pg. 481.

7. From the Brigade Record Book of Gen. Jacob D. Cox, in the manuscript collections of Oberlin College, Oberlin, Ohio, pgs. 286-87, book covers the period of May-November 1861.

8. From a letter published in the *Richmond Enquirer*, Oct. 1, 1861.

9. *Official Records*, V. 51, pt. 2, pg. 302.

10. *Ibid.*, V. 5, pgs. 861-63.

11. *Ibid.*, pg. 862.

12. *Ibid.*, pgs. 860-61.

13. From the unpublished diary of William Clark Reynolds, 22nd Virginia Infantry,

in the manuscript collections of the West Virginia State Archives, Charleston, W.Va.

14. *Official Records*, V. 51, pt. 2, pg. 304.

15. From an article published in the *Richmond Dispatch*, Richmond, Va., Sept. 25, 1861.

16. *Official Records*, V. 5, pg. 868.

17. *Ibid.*

18. "General Lee on Sewell Mountain," from *The Southern Bivouac*, January 1883, Number 5, pg. 182.

19. *Official Records*, V. 5, pg. 162.

20. *Ibid.*, V. 51, pt. 1, pg. 486.

21. *Ibid.*, V. 5, pg. 874.

22. *Ibid.*, pgs. 873-74.

23. *Ibid.*, pg. 878.

24. *Ibid.*, pgs. 878-79.

25. From the unpublished papers of Gen. Robert E. Lee, in the manuscript collec tions of the Virginia Historical Society, Richmond, Va., microfilm reel B55, Mss31515b- letter of Sept. 24, 1861.

26. *Ibid.*, another letter of Sept. 24, 1861.

27. *Southern Bivouac*, pg. 182.

28. *Official Records*, V., 51, pt. 2, pg. 312.

29. From the unpublished records of the Army of the Kanawha, in the manuscript collections of Duke University, Durham, N.C.

30. National Archives, Record Group 109, Records of the Army of the Kanawha, Chapter 2, V. 323, orders sent by Gen. Henry A. Wise, Special Orders Number 234, Sept. 25, 1861.

31. Charles T. Quintard, *Dr. Quintard, Chaplain C.S.A. and the Second Bishop of Tennessee*, A.M. Nell, ed., Sewanee, Tenn.: 1905, pg. 32.

32. From the *Report of the Joint Committee on the Conduct of the War*, testimony of Gen. William S. Rosecrans, Government Printing Office, Washington, D.C.: 1865, pg. 10.

33. J.M. Miller, *Recollections of a Pine Knot, Campaigns of West Virginia, Kentucky and Fort Donelson*, Commonwealth Publishing Co., Greenwood, Mississippi: 1899, pg. 7.

34. Robert E. Lee Jr., *Recollections and Letters of General Robert E. Lee*, New York: 1904, pgs. 48-9.

35. From the Civil War diary of E. Rockwell, 15th Indiana Infantry, in the manu script collections of the Indiana Historical Soceity, Indianapolis, Ind., pg. 16.

36. From an unsigned letter to the editor of the *Nashville Union and American*, Oct. 2, 1861., original in the manuscript collections of the Tennessee State Archives, Nashville, Tenn.

37. From the papers of Thomas Penn, in the manuscript collections of Duke University, Durham, N.C.

38. Letter of G.A. Cox, 8th Virginia Cavalry, Sept. 21, 1861, in the personal collection of Mr. John Alderman, Roanoke, Va.

39. Rutherford B. Hayes, Charles R. Williams, ed., *Diary and Letters of Rutherford B. Hayes*, Ohio State Archeological and Historical Society, Columbus, Ohio: 1922,

pgs. 103-04.

40. *Official Records*, V. 51, pt. 2, pg. 230.

41. Walter H. Taylor, *Four Years With General Lee*, Indiana University Press, reprint 1962, pg. 35.

42. Hayes, *Diary and Letters of Rutherford B. Hayes*, pg. 103.

43. *Official Records*, V. 51, pt. 2, pg. 324.

44. *Ibid.*, pgs. 325-26.

45. From a soldier's letter published in the *Cincinnati Daily Enquirer*, Oct. 1, 1861.

46. From the unpublished memoirs of W.S. Powell, 14th North Carolina Infantry, in the manuscript collections of the Southern Historical Society, deposited with the University of North Carolina, Chapel Hill, N.C.

47. From the Buford Family papers, in the manuscript collections of the University of Virginia, Charlottesville, Va.

48. Papers of Robert E. Lee, Virginia Historical Society.

49. Jacob D. Cox, pgs. 122-24.

50. National Archives, Records of the Adjutant Generals Office, Record Group 94, microcopy publication M 1098, Roll Number 6: The postwar papers of Gen. Henry Benham, 1873.

51. From the papers of Fleming Saunders, in the manuscript collections of the University of Virginia, Charlottesville, Va., letter of Oct. 7, 1861.

52. From the *Richmond Examiner*, Oct. 11, 1861.

53. J. Cutler Andrews, ed., *The South Reports the Civil War*, University of Pittsburg Press, reprint 1985.

54. Robert E. Lee Jr., Lee's letter of Oct. 7, 1861.

Chapter Nine

1. William D. Hamilton, *Recollections of a Cavalryman of the Civil War After Fifty Years*, F.J. Heer Printing Co., Columbus, Ohio: 1915, pg. 18.

2. From the letters of Gen. John T. Wilder, 17th Indiana Infantry, contained in the *Indiana Magazine of History*, V. 29, Bloomington, Ind.: 1933.

3. *Official Records*, V. 5, pg. 224.

4. John Henry Cammack, *Personal Recollections of Private John Henry Cammack: A Soldier of the Confederacy 1861-1865*, Paragon Printing Co., Huntington, W.Va.: 1920, pg. 38.

5. Barbara A. Smith, ed., *The Civil War Letters of Col. Elijah H.C. Cavins, 14th Indiana*, Cook-McDowell Publications, Owensboro, Ky.: 1981. (These letters were compiled from the originals which are included in the manuscript collections of the Indiana Historical Society, Indianapolis, Ind.)

6. Ann S. Stephens, *Pictorial History of the War for the Union*, James R. Hawley Publishers, Cincinnati, Ohio: 1863, pg. 190.

7. From the letters of Sergeant Shepherd Green Pryor, 12th Georgia Infantry, as published in the *Georgia Review*, V. 15, Number 1, University of Georgia Press, Athens, Ga.: 1961, pgs. 3-8.

8. From the letters of Basil Boyce, included in the papers of Leonard Perry, in the manuscript collections of the Indiana Historical Society, Indianapolis, Ind. (7th Ind. Inf.)

9. From letters contained in an unidentified newspaper clipping included among the Kirkpatrick Family papers, 32nd Ohio Volunteer Militia, in the manuscript collections of the Indiana Historical Society, Indianapolis, Ind.

10. Additional information on the death of Colonel Washington can be found in *Fourth Annual Reunion of the Fifteenth Indiana Volunteers*; reunion report, privately printed, Valparaiso, Ind.: 1889, pg. 12.

11. From the letters of W.S. Hord, 32nd Ohio Infantry, in the manuscript collec tions of the Ohio Historical Society, Columbus, Ohio.

12. *Georgia Review*, Pryor letters.

13. From the military letterbook of Gen. W.W. Loring, in the microfilm collections of the West Virginia and Regional History Library, Colson Hall, WVU, Morgantown.

Chapter Ten

1. *Official Records*, V. 5, pg. 615.

2. *Ibid.*

3. *Ibid.*, pg. 616.

4. *Ibid.*, pg. 899.

5. *Ibid.*, V. 51, pt. 2, pg. 347.

6. *Ibid.*, pgs. 348-49.

7. *Ibid.*, V. 5, pgs. 908-09.

8. From the unpublished papers of Gen. Robert E. Lee, 1861, in the manuscript collections of the Virginia Historical Society, Richmond, Va.

9. *Official Records*, V. 5, pg. 912.

10. Pvt. Adam Johnson, 3rd Regiment, Floyd Brigade, wrote on Oct. 23, 1861, that the move to Meadow Bluff was a good one, in that they had a better camping place with "wood & water plenty." Letter included in the manuscript collec tions of the West Virginia and Regional History Library, Colson Hall, WVU, Morgantown.

11. *Official Records*, V. 5, pg. 625.

12. *Ibid.*, pg. 638.

13. *Ibid.*, pg. 924.

14. *Ibid.*, V. 51, pt. 2, pg. 360.

15. *Ibid.*, pgs. 361-62.

16. Walter H. Taylor, *Four Years With General Lee*, Indiana University Press, reprint 1962, pgs. 34-5.

17. Tim McKinney, *The Civil War in Fayette County West Virginia*, Pictorial Histories Pub. Co., Charleston, W.Va.: 1988, pg. 123.

18. From the letters of J. Pinnick, 32nd Ohio Infantry, in the manuscript collections of the West Virginia and Regional History Library, Colson Hall, WVU, Morgantown.

19. Capt. I. Hermann, *Memoirs of a Veteran Who Served as a Private in the 60's in the War Between the States*, Byrd Printing Co., Atlanta, Ga.: 1911, pgs. 54-5. (1st Ga. Inf.)

20. "A Foot Soldier's Account: Letters of William Batts," as published in *The Georgia Historical Quarterly*, V. 50, 1966, pg. 91.

21. Official reports are contained in the *Official Records*, V. 5, pgs. 456-68.
22. Ambrose Bierce and William McCann, ed., *Ambrose Bierce's Civil War*, Gateway Editions, Inc., Chicago. Ill.: 1956, pg. 8.

TO THE PEOPLE

Of the Department of the KANAWHA VALLEY, embracing the following Counties, viz: Mason, Jackson, Putnam, Cabell, Wayne, Logan, Kanawha, Boone, Wyoming, Raleigh, Fayette, Nicholas and Clay: According to the following order, by the

Governor of Virginia:

Executive Department, April 29, 1861.

LIEUT. COL. McCAUSLAND:

Sir: You will proceed at once to the Kanawha Valley and assume command of the volunteer forces in that section, and organize and muster the same into the service of the State; and as soon as they are formed into Battalions or Regiments, report the fact to me, with the names of the company officers, the number of men in each company, and the kind and quality of arms.

Gen. Lee will give all necessary orders for your government in that command. I am very respectfully,
JOHN LETCHER.

I have arrived here to take command of the Department. I have instructions to call into the field ten companies, and one company of artillery. These troops will be encamped in the Kanawha Valley, near Buffalo, Putnam Co. They are intended for the protection of the Department; and I appeal to the people of the border counties to abstain from anything which will arouse ill feeling on either side of the Ohio river. This Department is organized by the proper authority in the State, and is provided with the credit to sustain itself; but for complete success, I firmly rely on the friendly disposition of the people therein.

The volunteer companies of the counties of Mason, Jackson and Putnam, will rendezvous at BUFFALO, Putnam Co.

The volunteer companies of the counties of Cabell, Wayne, and Logan, will rendezvous at BARBOURSVILLE, Cabell county.

The volunteer companies of the counties of Kanawha, Boone, Wyoming, Raleigh, Fayette, Nicholas and Clay, will rendezvous at CHARLESTON, Kanawha county.

The Captain of the volunteer companies in the above counties will remain at their respective drill grounds, until ordered to their rendezvous by the Commandant of the Department. So soon as preparation to receive them can be made, the companies will be ordered to their respective rendezvous, mustered into the service of the State, and then ordered to the Camp of Instruction. No company will be mustered into service unless it has at least 82 men.

The Captains will see that each man is provided with a uniform, one blanket, one haversack, one extra pair of shoes, two flannel shirts (to be worn in the place of the ordinary shirts), two pairs of drawers, four pairs of woolen socks, four handkerchiefs, towels, one comb and brush and tooth-brush, two pairs white gloves, one pair of rough pantaloons for fatigue duty, needles, thread, wax, buttons, &c., in a small buckskin bag. The whole (excepting the blanket) will be placed in a bag, this bag will be placed on the blanket and rolled up, and be secured to the back of each man by two straps.
Lt. Col. JNO. McCAUSLAND,
Commanding Dep't Ka. Valley.

BIBLIOGRAPHY

Books

Andrews, J. Cutler, ed., *The South Reports the Civil War*. University of Pitts
burgh Press, reprint, 1985.

Baxter, Nancy N., ed., *Hoosier Farmboy in Lincoln's Army: The Civil War
Letters of John R. McClure*. Privately printed, 1969.

_____, *Gallant Fourteenth: The Story of an Indiana Civil War Regiment*. India
napolis, Ind., The Guild Press, 1980 (paperback edition, 1986).

Bierce, Ambrose, William McCann, ed., *Ambrose Bierce's Civil War*. Chicago,
Ill., Gateway Editions, Inc., 1956.

Cammack, John Henry, *Personal Recollections of Private John Henry Cammack:
A Soldier of the Confederacy 1861-1865*. Huntington, W.Va., Paragon Printing
Company, 1920.

Chamberlayne, C.G., ed., *Ham Chamberlayne—Virginian: Letters and Papers of
an Artillery Officer*. Richmond, Va., The Deitz Printing Company, 1932.

Collier, Calvin L., *They'll Do To Tie To! The Story of the Third Regiment
Arkansas Infantry C.S.A.* Little Rock, Ark., Pioneer Press, 1959.

Cox, Jacob D., *Military Reminiscences*. New York, Charles Scribner & Sons,
1900.

Curry, Richard Orr, A House Divided. Pittsburg, Penna., University of Pitts
burgh Press, 1964.

Cutchins, John A., *A Famous Command: The Richmond Light Infantry Blues*.
Richmond, Va., Garrett & Massie, 1934.

Dowdey, Clifford and Louis H. Manarin, ed., *The Wartime Papers of Robert E.
Lee*. New York, Da Capo Press, 1987 (paperback reprint).

Drake, James V. *Life of General Robert Hatton*. Nashville, Tenn., Marshall &
Bruce, 1867.

Engle, Stephen D., *Thunder in the Hills*. Charleston, W.Va., Mountain State
Press, 1989.

Evans, Clement A., ed., *Confederate Military History*. 12 volumes, Atlanta, Ga.,
Confederate Pub. Co., 1899.

Freeman, Douglas S., *Robert E. Lee: A Biography*. New York, 1934-35.

Hamilton, William D., *Recollections of a Cavalryman of the Civil War After Fifty
Years*. Columbus, Ohio, F.J. Heer Printing Company, 1915.

Haselberger, Fritz, *Yanks From the South!* Baltimore, Md., Past Glories Press,
1987.

Hayes, Rutherford B. and Charles R. Williams, ed., *Diary and Letters of Rutherford B. Hayes*. Columbus, Ohio, Ohio State Archeological and Histori cal Society, 1922.

Head, Thomas A., *Campaigns and Battles of the 16th Regiment Tennessee Volunteers*. Nashville, Tenn., Cumberland Presbyterian Pub. House, 1885.

Hermann, I. (Captain), *Memoirs of a Veteran Who Served as a Private in the 60's in the War Between the States*. Atlanta, Ga., Byrd Printing Company, 1911.

Huckaby, Elizabeth Paisley and Ethel C. Simpson, ed., *Tulip Evermore: Emma Butler and William Paisley Their Lives in Letters, 1857-1887*. Fayetteville, Ark., University of Arkansas Press, 1985.

Keifer, Joseph Warren, *Slavery and Four Years of War*. New York and London, G.P. Putnam's Sons, 1900.

Lang. Theodore F., *Loyal West Virginia From 1861-1865*. Baltimore, Md., Deutch Pub. Co., 1895.

Lee, Robert E. Jr., *Recollections and Letters of General Robert E. Lee*. New York, 1904.

Linger, James C., *Confederate Military Units of West Virginia*. Tulsa, Okla., privately printed ,1992.

Lowry, Terry, *The Battle of Scary Creek*. Charleston, W.Va., Pictorial Histories Pub. Co., 1982.

_____, *September Blood: The Battle of Carnifex Ferry*. Charleston, W.Va., Pictorial Histories Pub. Co., 1985.

McClellan, George B., *Report on the Organization and Campaigns of the Army of the Potomac*. New York, 1864.

_____, *McClellan's Own Story*. New York, 1887.

McKinney, Tim, *The Civil War in Fayette County West Virginia*. Charleston, W.Va., Pictorial Histories Pub. Co., 1988.

_____, *Robert E. Lee at Sewell Mountain: The West Virginia Campaign*. Charles ton, W.Va., Pictorial Histories Pub. Co., 1990.

_____, *Civil War Articles in the Fayette Tribune, 1907-1936, An Annotated Index*. Fayetteville, W.Va., Privately printed booklet, 1991.

Merrill, Catherine, *The Soldier of Indiana in the War For the Union*. Indianapo lis, Ind., Merrill & Co., 1866.

Miller, J.M., *Recollections of a Pine Knot: Campaigns of West Virginia, Kentucky and Fort Donelson*. Greenwood, Miss., Commonwealth Pub. Co., 1899.

Pinkerton, Allan, *Spy of the Rebellion*. New York, 1883.

Pool, J.T., *Under Canvas; or Recollections of the Fall and Summer Campaign of the 14th Regiment, Indiana Volunteers*.

Price, William T., *Historical Sketches of Pocahontas County, West Virginia*. Marlinton, W.Va., Price Brothers Publisher, 1901.

Quintard, Charles T., *Dr. Quintard: Chaplain C.S.A. and Second Bishop of Tennessee*. Sewanee, Tenn., A.H. Noll, 1905.

Reid, Whitelaw and James G. Smart, ed., *A Radical View: The "Agate" Dis patches of Whitelaw Reid 1861-1865*. Memphis, Tenn., Memphis State University Press, 1976 (2 volumes).

Rice, Otis K., *A History of Greenbrier County West Virginia*. Parson, W.Va., McClain Printing Co., 1986.

Smith, Barbara A., ed., *The Civil War Letters of Col. Elijah H.C. Cavins, 14th Indiana*. Owensboro, Ky., Cook-McDowell Publications, 1981.

Steiner, Paul E., *Disease in the Civil War: Biological Warfare in 1861-1865*. Springfield, Ill., Charles C. Thomas Publisher, 1968.

Stephens, Ann S., *Pictorial History of the War For the Union*. Cincinnati, Ohio, James R. Hawley Publisher, 1863.

Stutler, Boyd, *The Civil War in West Virginia*. Charleston, W.Va., Education Foundation, 1963.

Tavel, Albert B., *Cheat Mountain: or, Unwritten Chapter of the Late War*. Nashville, Tenn., A.B. Tavel, printer, 1885.

Taylor, Walter H., *Four Years With General Lee*. New York, D. Appleton Company, 1878 (reprint, Bloomington, Ind., Indiana University Press, 1962).

_____, *General Lee, His Campaigns in Virginia 1861-1865*. Norfolk, 1906 (reprint, Dayton, Ohio, Morningside Bookshop, 1975).

Toney, Marcus B., *The Privations of a Private*. Nashville, Tenn., Privately printed, 1905.

United States War Department, *Report of the Joint Committee on the Conduct of the War*. Washington, D.C., Government Printing Office, 1865.

_____, *War of the Rebellion: A Compilation of the Official Records of the Union & Confederate Armies*. Washington, D.C., Government Printing Office, 1881-1901, 70 volumes in 128 books.

Virginia, Commonwealth of, *Journal of the Senate of the Commonwealth of Virginia, 1861, Extra Session*. Richmond, Va., 1861.

Watkins, Samuel R., *Co. Aytch Maury Grays, First Tennessee Regiment*. Nashville, Tenn., Cumberland Presbyterian Publishing House, 1882.

Wise, John S., *End of an Era*. New York, A.S. Barnes and Company, 1965.

Womack, Walter, ed., *The Civil War Diary of Captain J.J. Womack, Co. E. 16th Tennessee Volunteers*. McMinnville, Tenn., Womack Printing Company, 1961.

Worsham, John H., *One of Jackson's Foot Cavalry*. Jackson, Tenn., McCowat-Mercer Press Inc., 1964.

Zinn, Jack, *R.E. Lee's Cheat Mountain Campaign*. Parsons, W.Va., McClain Printing Company, 1974.

Books Secondary

Ambler, Charles H., *Francis H. Pierpont, Union War Governor of Virginia and Father of West Virginia*. Chapel Hill, N.C., University of North Carolina Press, 1937.

Brown, Stephen W., *Voice of the New West: John G. Jackson, His Life and Times*. Macon, Ga., Mercer University Press, 1985.

Cohen, Stan, *A Pictorial Guide to West Virginia's Civil War Sites*. Charleston, W.Va., Pictorial Histories Pub. Co., 1990.

_____, *The Civil War in West Virginia A Pictorial History*, Charleston, W.Va., Pictorial Histories Pub. Co., 1976.

Geiger, Joe Jr., *Civil War in Cabell County West Virginia 1861-1865*. Charleston, W.Va., Pictorial Histories Pub. Co., 1991.

Grebner, Constantine, *We Were the Ninth*. Kent, Ohio, Kent State University Press, 1987 (English language version of the original 1897 publication which was in German).

Hall, Granville D., *The Rending of Virginia*. Chicago, Ill., Mayer & Miller Press, 1901.

Heth, Henry and James L. Morrison, ed., *The Memoirs of Henry Heth*. Westport, Conn., Greenwood Press, 1974.

Humphreys, Milton W., *Military Operations 1861-1864*. Fayetteville, W.Va., Privately printed, 1926 (reprint edition, Gauley Bridge, W.Va., Thomas In-Prints, 1991).

Kellogg, Sanford C., The Shenandoah Valley of Virginia 1861-1865. New York, The Neale Publishing Co., 1903.

Krick, Robert K., *Lee's Colonels: A Biographical Register of the Field Officers of the Army of Northern Virginia*. Dayton, Ohio, Morningside Press, (4th edition), 1992.

Lamers, William A., *The Edge of Glory: A Biography of Gen. William S. Rosecrans*. New York, Harcourt—Brace & World, 1961.

Maxwell, Hu, *The History of Randolph County West Virginia*. Morgantown, W.Va., Acme Publishing Co., 1898.

Moore, George E., *A Banner in the Hills*. New York, Appleton-Century-Crofts, 1963.

Pauley, Michael J., *Unreconstructed Rebel: The Life of General John McCausland C.S.A.*, Charleston, W.Va., Pictorial Histories Publishing Co., 1993.

Seventeenth Indiana Regiment, *Souvenir of the 17th Indiana Regiment: A History From Its Organization to the End of the War*. Terre Haute, Ind., 17th Regt. Reunion Organization, 1889.

Skidmore, Richard S., ed., *The Civil War Journal of Billy Davis: From Hopewell, Indiana to Port Republic, Virginia*. Greencastle, Ind., The Nuggett Publishers, 1989.

Summers, Festus P., *A Borderland Confederate*. Pittsburgh, Penna., University of Pittsburgh Press, 1962.

Terrell, W.H.H., *Indiana in the War of the Rebellion*. Indianapolis, Ind., Indiana Historical Bureau, 1960.

Whittlesey, Charles, *War Memoranda: Cheat River to the Tennessee 1861-1862*. Cleveland, Ohio, 1884.

Winters, Joshua and Elizabeth D. Swiger, ed., *Civil War Letters and Diary of Joshua Winters*. (1st W.Va. Inf.), Parsons, W.Va., McClain Printing Company, 1991.

(The author also utilized to some extent the various regimental histories included in the *Virginia Regimental Histories Series* being published by H.E. Howard, Inc., Lynchburg, Va.)

Magazines and Journals

Commandery of the State of Illinois, Military Order of the Loyal Legion of the United States. "Lee's Advance and Retreat in the Cheat Mt. Campaign in

1861." By Col. John Levering, published in "Military Essays and Recollec
tions," volume 4, 1907.

Confederate Veteran Magazine, "Mother to the First Tennessee Regiment,"
Vol. 34, August 1926.

____, "The Mountain Campaign Failure," by A.C. Jones, Vol. 22, 1914.

Georgia Historical Quarterly, "A Foot Soldier's Account: Letters of William
Batts," Vol. 50, 1966.

Georgia Review, "The Letters of Sgt. Shepherd Green Pryor, 12th Georgia
Infantry," Vol. 15, Number 1, 1961.

Histories and Battalions From North Carolina in the Great War 1861-1865,
"Additional Sketch Sixteenth Regiment," by B.H. Cathey, Vol. 4.

Indiana Magazine of History, "The Letters of General John T. Wilder, 17th
Indiana Infantry," Vol. 29, 1933.

Jackson County (W.Va.) *Miscellany*, "Memoir of a Youthful Confederate,"
West   Virginia Historical Society.

Randolph County Historical Society Magazine of History and Biography,
"George W. Peterkin at Valley Mountain," by Eva M. Carnes, Vol. 12, 1961.

Southern Bivouac, "General Lee on Sewell Mountain," Vol. Number 5,
January 1883.

West Virginia Review, "The Journal of a Soldier of 1861," by W.C. Clark,
November 1930.

Magazines and Journals Secondary

Confederate Veteran Magazine (*CVM*) in order of date:
  "Scouting in West Virginia," July 1894, pg. 214.
  "A Battle Planned But Not Fought," June 1897, pg. 293.
  "Lee and Traveller," June 1898, pg. 292.
  "Gen. R.E. Lee at Cheat Mountain," March 1899, pg. 116.
  "Monument at Valley Mountain," September 1902, pg. 388.
  "Thrilling Experiences of Lieut. Col. Lang," November 1905, pg. 497.
  "Trainer of Traveller—Frank Paige," December 1907, pg. 548.
  "The Cheat Mountain Campaign," March 1915, pg. 122.
  "The Story of a Five-Dollar Gold Piece," February 1916, pg. 76.
  "Col. John A. Washington, C.S.A.," July 1922, pg. 245.
  "Col. John Augustine Washington, C.S.A.," March 1926, pg. 96.
  "When Colonel Washington was Killed," May 1926, pg. 169.
  "Letters on the West Virginia Campaigns," June 1926, pg. 216.
  "The First West Virginia Campaigns," May 1930, pg. 186.

Magazine of the Jefferson County (WV) Historical Society, "Death of Wash
ington," (Lee's aide), December 1961.

United Daughters of the Confederacy Magazine, "Colonel John Augustine
Washington C.S.A.," March 1991, pg. 14-16.

West Virginia History Magazine (*WVH*) in order of date:
  "The Campaigns of McClellan & Rosecrans in West Virginia," July 1944.
  "General John B. Floyd and the West Virginia Campaigns of 1861," April

1947.

"Conflicting Interpretations as to the Causes of the Civil War," October 1961.

"The Mind of a Copperhead: Letters of John J. Davis on the Secession Crisis and Statehood Politics in Western Virginia 1860-1862," January 1963.

"Lincoln and West Virginia Statehood," July 1963.

"The Presidential Election of 1860 in West Virginia," April 1964.

Newspapers and Articles

Cincinnati Daily Enquirer, Oct. 1, 1861, unsigned soldier letter.

Herald-Courier, Bristol, Tenn., "The War Story of a Confederate Soldier Boy," published between Jan. 23 and Feb. 27, 1921.

Indianapolis Journal, Aug. 8, 1861, unsigned letter dated Aug. 1, 1861, at foot of Cheat Mountain, Va.

Indianapolis Journal, Aug. 14, 1861, unsigned letter dated Aug. 7, 1861, at Huttonsville, Va.

Indianapolis Journal, Sept. 5, 1861, unsigned letter dated Aug. 28, 1861, at Cheat Mountain, Va.

Nashville Union & American, Nashville, Tenn., Oct. 11, 1861, unsigned letter dated Oct. 2, 1861, at Sewell Mountain, Va.

Richmond Dispatch, Richmond, Va., "The Situation in West Virginia," published Sept. 25, 1861.

Richmond Dispatch, Richmond, Va., Sept. 27, 1861, unsigned letter to the editor of the *Atlanta Confederacy* by a member of the 1st Georgia Infantry dated Sept. 18, 1861, at Camp Bartow, Va.

Richmond Enquirer, Richmond, Va., Oct. 1, 1861, unsigned letter to the editor.

Wheeling Intelligencer, Wheeling, Va., unidentified article on the statehood movement, published Feb. 4, 1861, and updated on April 26, 1861.

Newspapers and Articles Secondary

Belington News, Belington, W.Va., "Place of Evil Spirits," (Lee in W.Va.), June 3, 1959.

Belington News, Issues of June 3, 10, and 17, 1959, contain a series on the Civil War in West Virginia by Eva M. Carnes.

Charleston Gazette, Charleston, W.Va., "When Lee Failed to Fight," (Cheat Mt.), Feb. 3, 1957.

Charleston Gazette, Charleston, W.Va., "Death of Lee's Aide," (Col. Washington), Nov. 30, 1958.

Clarksburg Sunday Exponent Telegram, Clarksburg, W.Va., "Old Randolph Countian Recalls Civil War," April 6, 1941.

Fairmont Times, Fairmont, W.Va., "Tygart Valley Was Scene of Action," April 16, and April 29, 1962.

Fayette Tribune, Fayetteville, W.Va., "General Lee's Old War Horse," (Traveller), by T. Broun, Jan. 24, 1907.

Fayette Tribune, "Lee's Campaign in West Virginia," (Cheat and Valley Mt.), Aug. 18, 1921.

Pocahontas Times, Marlinton, W.Va., editorial concerning "Traveler's Re pose," at Bartow, W.Va., Jan. 25, 1940.

Wheeling News Register, Wheeling, W.Va., "Lee Fails in West Virginia," an article by Boyd B. Stutler, March 22, 1959.

Manuscripts and Narratives

Army of the Kanawha, unpublished records in the manuscript collections of Duke University, Durham, N.C.

Army of the Kanawha, unpublished records in the National Archives, Record Group 109, Army of the Kanawha, Chapter 2, Vol. 323, orders sent by Gen. Henry A. Wise.

Papers of Lieut. D.B. Baldwin (51st Va. Inf.) in the manuscript collections of the Virginia Historical Society, Richmond, Va.

Postwar papers of Gen. Henry Benham, National Archives Records of the Adj. Generals Office, Record Group 94, microcopy publication M 1098, Roll #6 (1873).

Buford Family papers, Capt. John C. Buford, 42nd Va. Inf., in the manuscript collections of the University of Virginia, Charlottesville.

Diary of Carroll Clark, 16th Tennessee Infantry, in the manuscript collections of the Tennessee State Archives, Nashville.

Letters of G.A. Cox, 8th Va. Cavalry, in the personal collection of Mr. John Alderman, Roanoke, Va.

Brigade Record Book of Gen. Jacob D. Cox, in the manuscript collections of Oberlin College, Oberlin, Ohio.

Diary of Mary Fontaine (concerning her sons service with the 21st Va. Inf.), in the manuscript collections of the University of Charleston, Charleston, W.Va.. Copy provided courtesy of Dr. Otis K. Rice, via the Mountain State Press.

Papers of John Halvey, 13th Indiana Infantry, in the manuscript collections of the Indiana Historical Society, Indianapolis.

Papers of William F. Harrison, 23rd Virginia Infantry, in the manuscript collections of Duke University, Durham, N.C.

Papers of Richard N. Hewitt, 42nd Virginia Infantry, in the manuscript collections of Duke University, Durham, N.C.

Papers of W.S. Hord, 32nd Ohio Volunteer Infantry, in the manuscript collections of the Ohio Historical Society, Columbus, Ohio.

Papers of Adam Johnson, 3rd Regiment Floyd Brigade, in the manuscript collections of the West Virginia and Regional History Library, Colson Hall, WVU Morgantown.

Kirkpatrick Family papers, Indiana Infantry, in the manuscript collections of the Indiana Historical Society, Indianapolis, Ind.

Journal of George Washington Lambert, 14th Indiana Infantry, in the manu script collections of the Indiana Historical Society, Indianapolis, Ind.

Unpublished papers of Robert E. Lee, in the manuscript collections of the

Virginia Historical Society, Richmond.

Letterbook of Gen. William Wing Loring, C.S.A., in the manuscript (micro film) collections of the West Virginia and Regional History Library, Colson Hall, WVU Morgantown.

Papers of Thomas Penn, 42nd Virginia Infantry, in the manuscript collections of Duke University, Durham, N.C.

Papers of Leonard Perry, 7th Indiana Infantry, in the manuscript collections of the Indiana Historical Society, Indianapolis, Ind.

Papers of the J. Pinnick, 32nd Ohio Infantry, in the manuscript collections of the West Virginia and Regional History Library, Colson Hall, WVU Morgantown.

Papers of W.S. Powell, 14th North Carolina Infantry, in the manuscript collections of the University of North Carolina, Chapel Hill, N.C.

Diary of William Clark Reynolds, 22nd Virginia Infantry, in the manuscript collections of the West Virginia Department of Archives and History, Charleston, W.Va.

Diary of E. Rockwell, 15th Indiana Infantry, in the manuscript colletions of the Indiana Historical Society, Indianapolis, Ind.

Papers of Flemming Saunders, 42nd Virginia Infantry, in the manuscript collections of the University of Virginia, Charlottesville.

Papers of Capt. Robert W. Snead, 50th Virginia Infantry, in the manuscript collections of the Virginia Historical Society, Richmond, Va.

Diary of Joseph C. Snider, 31st Virginia Infantry, in the manuscript collections of the West Virginia and Regional History Library, Colson Hall, WVU Morgantown.

Papers of the C.Q. Tompkins Family, 22nd Virginia Infantry, in the manuscript collections of the Virginia Historical Society, Richmond, Va.

Index

The author and his wife,
Brenda Humphrey McKinney,
married June 27, 1993.

About the Author

Tim McKinney is a native of Fayette County, West Virginia. He is active in a variety of historic preservation and tourism development organizations. This work is Mr. McKinney's fifth history publication, and his fourth book on the American Civil War. He is an employee of West Virginia Institute of Technology, Montgomery, W.Va. He can be reached via P.O. Box 266, Charlton Heights, W.Va. 25040.